Current Controversies in Macroeconomics

To Christine and Margaret

Current Controversies in Macroeconomics

An Intermediate Text

Howard R. Vane
and John L. Thompson
Liverpool Polytechnic

Edward Elgar

Published by
Edward Elgar Publishing Limited
Gower House
Croft Road
Aldershot
Hants GU11 3HR
England

Edward Elgar Publishing Limited
Distributed in the United States by Ashgate Publishing Company
Old Post Road
Brookfield
Vermont 05036
USA

A CIP catalogue record for this book is available from the British Library

Library of Congress Cataloging-in-Publication Data

Vane, Howard R.
Current controversies in macroeconomics: an intermediate text/ by Howard R. Vane and John L. Thompson.
p. cm.
Includes bibliographical references and index.
1. Macroeconomics. I. Thompson, John L. II. Title.
HB172.5.V35 1992
339-dc20 91-27099
CIP

ISBN 1 85278 089 4
1 85278 591 8 (paperback)

Printed in Great Britain by
Billing and Sons Ltd, Worcester

Contents

Figures

Preface

This book aims to provide a concise yet rigorous discussion of major issues in modern macroeconomics, in particular in relation to the controversy over the role and conduct of macroeconomic stabilization policy, for students taking intermediate-level undergraduate courses in macroeconomics.

While written in such a way as to allow students to read individual chapters in isolation, according to their interests and needs, the book follows a structured direction. After providing a review of mainstream macro-models and schools of thought in Chapter 1, subsequent chapters focus on selected key controversies surrounding the balance of payments and exchange rates (Chapter 2); inflation and unemployment (Chapter 3); money and economic activity (Chapter 4); fiscal policy and aggregate demand (Chapter 5) and business cycles (Chapter 6).

In preparing the book we would especially like to thank Jackie Lewis for her patience and co-operation in typing a substantial part of the final typescript. Any remaining errors are our responsibility.

Howard Vane and John Thompson

1. Mainstream Macro-Models and Schools of Thought

1.1 INTRODUCTION

The main purpose of this chapter is twofold. First to provide an introductory revision of the underlying structure and policy implications of the three most frequently employed textbook models of the macroeconomy. To this end we begin with a brief review of the essential elements of the Keynesian cross or 45° line model (section 1.2.1) before reviewing the IS-LM model (section 1.2.2) and finally the aggregate demand/supply model (section 1.2.3). Second, within this framework to summarize the main areas of controversy between Keynesian (section 1.3.1), monetarist (section 1.3.2), and new classical approaches (section 1.3.3) over the role and conduct of macroeconomic stabilization policy. This review will not only provide a useful introductory revision but will also help place particular controversies discussed in greater detail in subsequent chapters in the wider context of macroeconomic analysis you have already studied.

1.2 MAINSTREAM MACRO-MODELS

1.2.1 The Keynesian Cross or 45° Model

The simplest and most familiar textbook model of the macroeconomy is the fixed-price Keynesian cross or 45° line model. The essence of the model is that the level of output and employment is determined by aggregate demand/expenditure. Aggregate demand (AD) is comprised of the sum of consumption (C), investment (I), government expenditure (G) and net exports, i.e. exports minus imports (X − Im).

$$AD = C + I + G + X - Im \tag{1.1}$$

We now discuss a stylized representation of the main determinants of each of these individual components of aggregate demand. Consumption expenditure is held to depend positively on disposable income i.e. income (Y) minus taxes (T).

$$C = \alpha + \beta (Y - T) \tag{1.2}$$

In this function (equation 1.2) consumption is treated as a linear relationship with an autonomous element (α) and a constant marginal propensity to consume (β) which is greater than zero but less than one. Tax revenue (T) is assumed to be proportional to income i.e. the marginal tax rate is constant. The three main injections to the circular flow of income of investment (I), government expenditure (G) and gross exports (X) are all taken as being exogenously determined in that while they affect, they are not themselves affected by other variables in the model. Finally imports (Im) are assumed to be proportional to national income with a marginal propensity to import (m) greater than zero but less than one (equation 1.3).

$$Im = mY \tag{1.3}$$

The equilibrium level of national income/output (Y_0) occurs where aggregate demand equals aggregate supply. This is illustrated in Figure 1.1 where the aggregate demand schedule (AD_0) crosses or cuts the 45° line, a line which shows points of equality between the two axes of aggregate demand and national output. It is important to emphasize that the traditional assumption underlying this model is that unemployment exists so that any increase in aggregate demand can and will be met by an increase in output (aggregate supply). In other words supply constraints are ignored and the level of national income/output is entirely determined by aggregate demand. With the economy settling at a position of less than full employment equilibrium (i.e. at Y_0 in Figure 1.1) due to a deficiency of aggregate demand, interventionist policy is required in the form of an increase in government expenditure and/or a decrease in taxes in order to increase output towards its full employment level. This is illustrated in Figure 1.1. For example, *ceteris paribus*, an increase in government expenditure from G_0 to G_1 will shift the aggregate demand schedule upwards from AD_0 to AD_1 (ΔAD) and result in an increase in national income/output from Y_0 to Y_1 (ΔY). The extent to which the government decides to stimulate aggregate demand depends on the size of the multiplier. The multiplier itself depends on the size of all leakages from the circular flow of income and will be larger: (i) the greater the

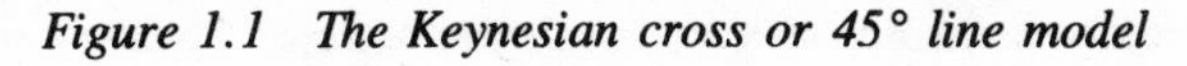

Figure 1.1 The Keynesian cross or 45° line model

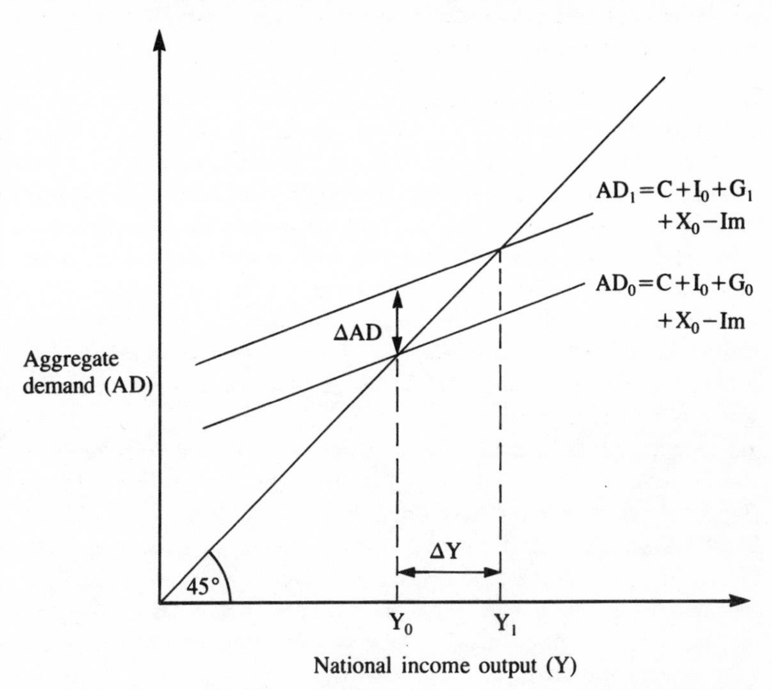

marginal propensity to consume; (ii) the smaller the marginal tax rate and (iii) the smaller the marginal propensity to import. In terms of Figure 1.1 the multiplier will be larger the steeper the slope of the aggregate demand schedule. In summary the main policy implication derived from the Keynesian cross or 45° line model is that fiscal policy changes can and, therefore, should, be used to maintain the economy at a high and stable level of employment.

We now turn to review the essential features and policy implications of the IS-LM model which incorporates a monetary sector into this simple expenditure model.

1.2.2 The IS-LM Model

The central feature of the fixed-price IS-LM model is the way in which the model integrates real and monetary factors in determining aggregate demand and therefore the level of output and employment. We begin our review of the model with the goods market and the IS curve.

The goods market and the IS curve

Equilibrium in the goods market occurs where the aggregate demand for and supply of goods are equal. As in the case of the fixed-price Keynesian cross or 45° line model, supply constraints are ignored and the level of output and employment is assumed to be determined entirely by aggregate demand. The main determinants of consumption, government expenditure and net exports are the same as those assumed in the simple expenditure model described in equations (1.1) to (1.3). The significant departure from that specification is that investment is treated as being inversely related to the rate of interest (a variable determined within the model) while also having an autonomous element which is treated as exogenous.

The IS curve traces out a locus of combinations of interest rates and income associated with equilibrium in the goods market (see Figure 1.2b). Given the assumption that investment is inversely related to the rate of interest the IS curve is downward sloping. *Ceteris paribus*, as the rate of interest falls investment increases, resulting in a higher level of national income (see Figure 1.2a). The slope of the IS curve depends on the responsiveness of investment to changes in the rate of interest and the value of the multiplier. The IS curve will be steeper the more investment expenditure is interest inelastic (unresponsive) and the smaller is the value of the multiplier. Conversely the IS curve will be flatter the more investment expenditure is interest elastic (responsive) and the greater is the value of the multiplier. For example, *ceteris paribus* the more investment increases for a given fall in the rate of interest the more national income will increase, generating a flatter IS curve. Finally it is important to note that expansionary fiscal policy (i.e. an increase in government expenditure and/or a reduction in taxation) shifts the IS curve outwards to the right. For example an increase in government expenditure will be associated with a higher level of national income at any given level of the rate of interest. The extent to which the IS curve shifts depends on the size of the multiplier, the outward shift being equal to the increase in government expenditure times the value of the multiplier.

Next we turn to the money market and the LM curve.

The money market and the LM curve

Equilibrium in the money market occurs where the demand for and supply of money are equal. The money supply is assumed to be exogenously

Figure 1.2 The IS curve

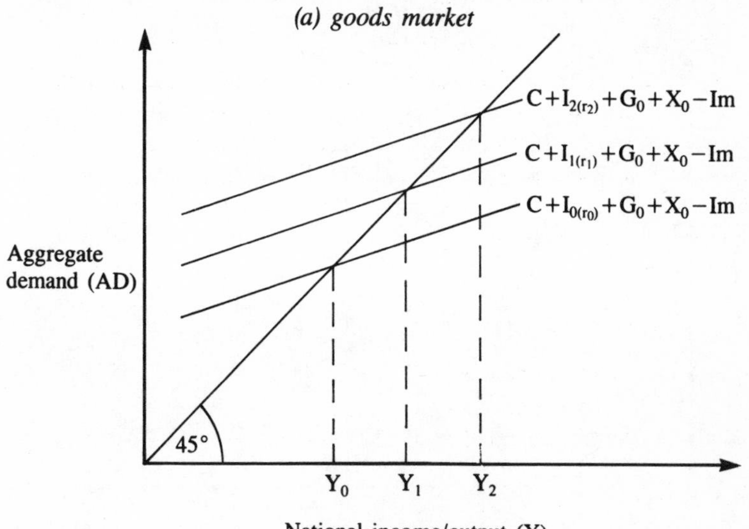

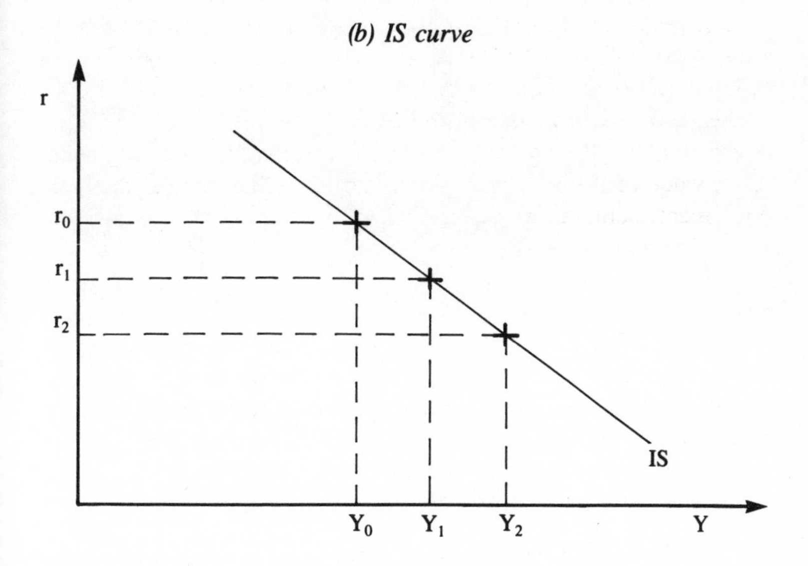

Figure 1.3 The LM curve

(a) Money market

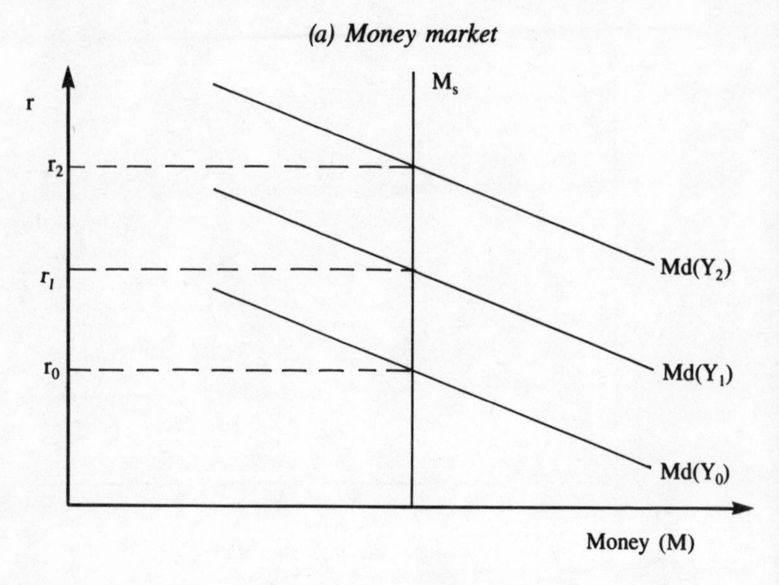

(b) LM curve

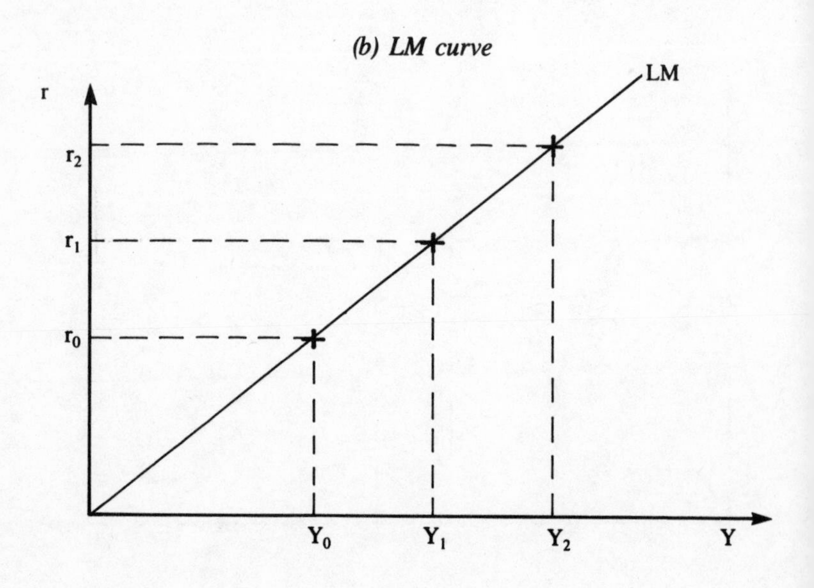

determined by the authorities while the demand for money varies positively with income (due to transactions and precautionary motives) and inversely with the rate of interest (due to the speculative motive). The LM curve traces out a locus of combinations of interest rates and income associated with equilibrium in the money market (see Figure 1.3b). Given the assumption that the demand for money increases with income and falls with the rate of interest the LM curve is upward sloping. *Ceteris paribus*, a higher level of national income must be associated with a higher rate of interest to maintain equilibrium in the money market (see Figure 1.3a). The slope of the LM curve depends on the responsiveness of the demand for money to changes in the level of national income and the rate of interest. The LM curve will be steeper the higher the income elasticity and the smaller the interest elasticity of the demand for money. Conversely the LM curve will be flatter the smaller the income elasticity and the greater the interest elasticity of the demand for money.

Expansionary monetary policy shifts the LM curve downwards to the

Figure 1.4 The IS-LM model

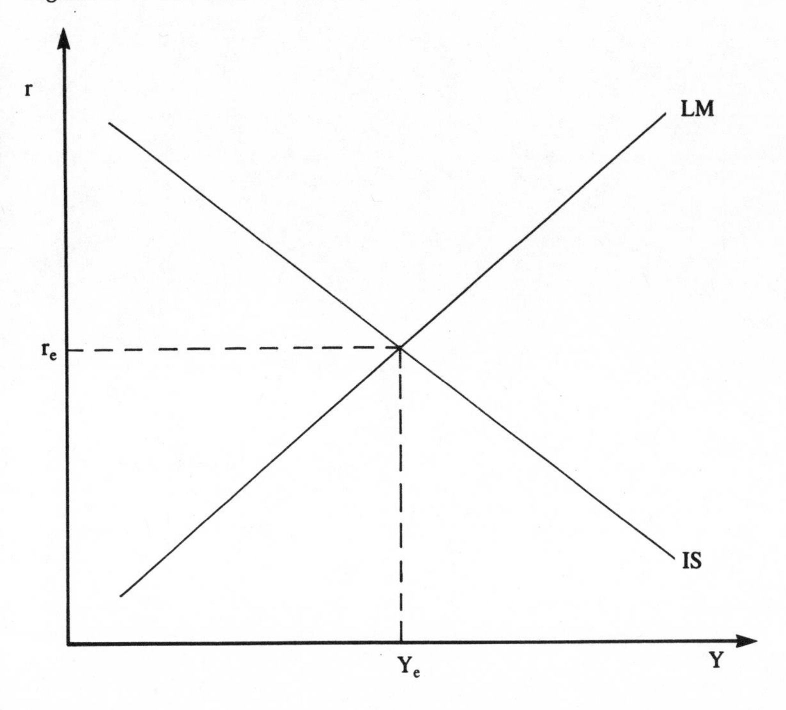

right. Following an increase in the money supply, and a given income elasticity of the demand for money, any given level of income must be associated with a lower rate of interest to maintain equilibrium in the money market. The extent to which the LM curve shifts depends on the interest elasticity of the demand for money. A given increase in the supply of money will cause a small/large shift in the LM curve where the demand for money is relatively interest elastic/inelastic as equilibrium in the money market will be restored by a small/large fall in the rate of interest.

Equilibrium in the goods and money market

Equilibrium in both the goods and the money market is simultaneously attained where the IS and LM curves intersect, i.e. at r_eY_e in Figure 1.4. Within the model both fiscal and monetary policy have an important role to play in influencing the level of output and employment. This is illustrated in Figures 1.5 and 1.6.

In Figure 1.5 the economy is initially in equilibrium at r_0Y_0 (i.e the intersection of IS_0 and LM). Expansionary fiscal policy shifts the IS

Figure 1.5 Expansionary fiscal policy

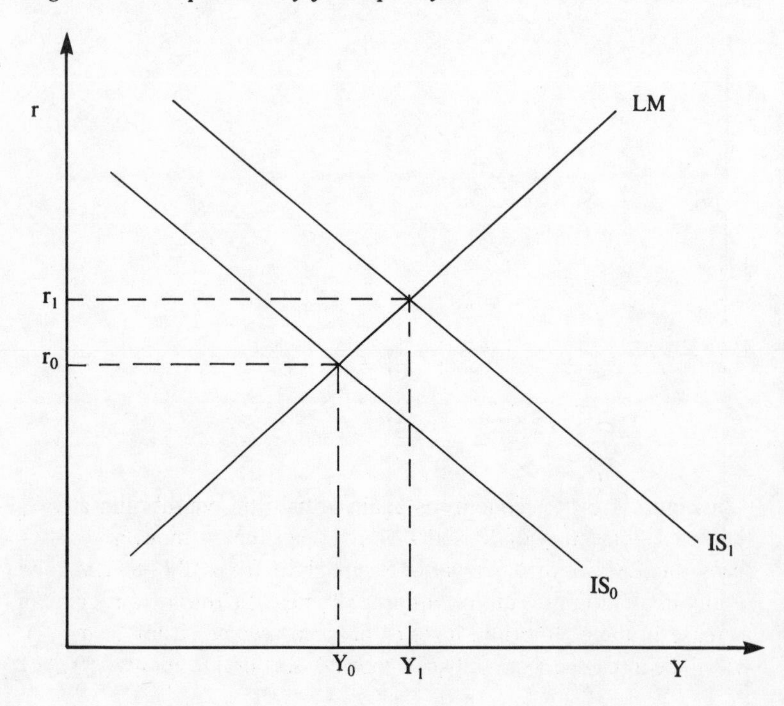

curve outwards to the right from IS_0 to IS_1 and results in an increase in both the equilibrium rate of interest (from r_0 to r_1) and the equilibrium level of national income (from Y_0 to Y_1). As will be discussed more fully in Chapter 5, section 5.2.1, fiscal policy will be more effective in influencing aggregate demand: (i) the more interest elastic is the demand for money (i.e. the flatter is the LM curve) and (ii) the less interest elastic is investment (i.e. the steeper is the IS curve).

Figure 1.6 Expansionary monetary policy

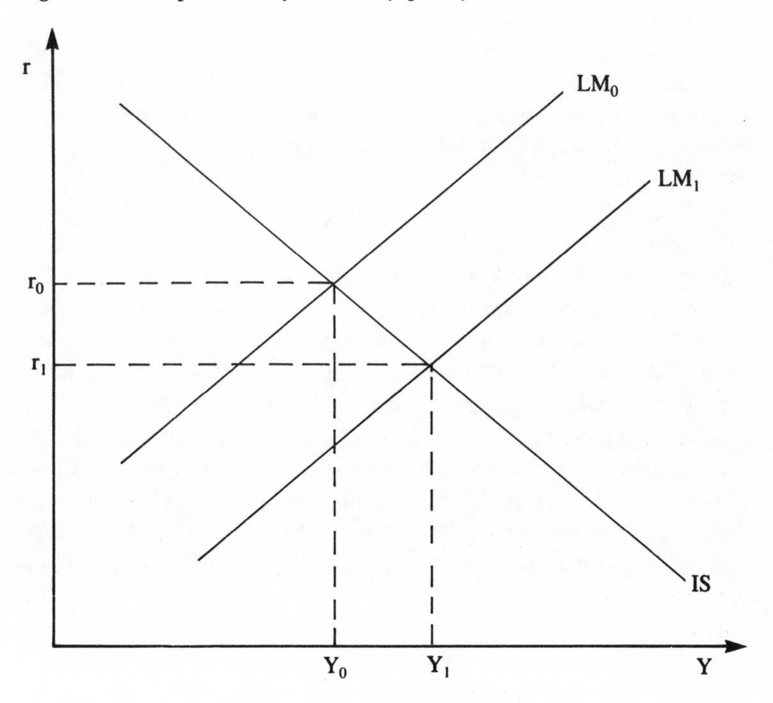

In Figure 1.6 the economy is again initially in equilibrium at r_0Y_0 (i.e. the intersection of IS and LM_0). Expansionary monetary policy shifts the LM curve downwards to the right from LM_0 to LM_1 and results in a fall in the equilibrium rate of interest (from r_0 to r_1) and an increase in the equilibrium level of national income (from Y_0 to Y_1). As will be discussed more fully in Chapter 4, section 4.2, monetary policy will be more effective in influencing aggregate demand: (i) the more interest inelastic is the demand for money (i.e. the steeper is the LM curve) and (ii) the more interest elastic is investment (i.e. the flatter is the IS curve). In summary the relative effectiveness of fiscal and monetary policy depends on the relative slopes of the IS and LM curves, i.e. on the structural parameters underlying the model.

1.2.3 The Aggregate Demand – Aggregate Supply Model

The two models we have considered so far focus entirely on the aggregate demand side of the economy and for analytical convenience treat the price level as exogenously given. We now consider a model which incorporates an aggregate supply side to the economy and in which the price level is endogenously determined. We begin with a review of the relationship between aggregate demand and the price level depicted in the aggregate demand curve.

The aggregate demand curve

The downward-sloping aggregate demand curve depicted in Figure 1.7b is easily derived from the IS-LM model. Reference to Figure 1.7a reveals that for a given IS curve and a given nominal money supply as the price level falls (from P_0 to P_1 to P_2) the real value of the nominal money supply increases (shifting the LM curve to the right) and the level of real income increases (from Y_0 to Y_1 to Y_2). The aggregate demand (AD) curve then traces out a locus of combinations of the price level and real income which are compatible with equilibrium in the IS-LM model. From this follows that the slope of the AD curve depends on the relative slopes of the IS and LM curves. The AD curve will be steeper (flatter) the flatter (steeper) the LM curve is and the steeper (flatter) the IS curve is. The reader should verify for himself/herself that in the two extreme Keynesian cases of a horizontal LM curve (liquidity trap) and a vertical IS curve (perfectly interest-inelastic investment) the AD curve will become vertical. It also follows from this analysis that: (a) for a given LM curve anything that shifts the IS curve to the right (e.g. expansionary fiscal policy) or (b) for a given IS curve anything that shifts the LM curve to the right (e.g. expansionary monetary policy) will shift the AD curve to the right, and vice versa. The reader should also verify for himself/herself that how far either expansionary fiscal or monetary policy shifts the AD curve to the right depends on the relative slopes of the IS and LM curves i.e. the structural parameters underlying the IS-LM model.

Figure 1.7 The aggregate demand curve

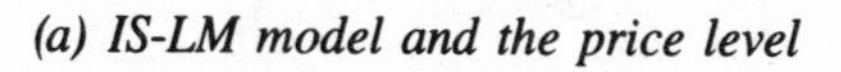

(a) IS-LM model and the price level

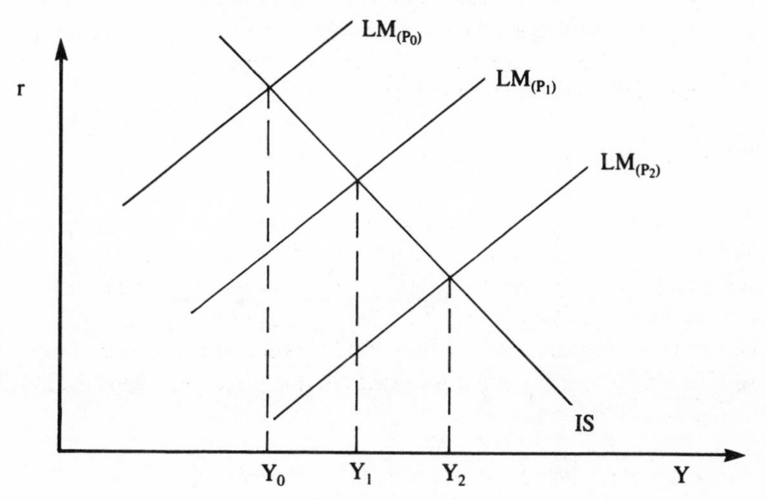

(b) Aggregate demand curve

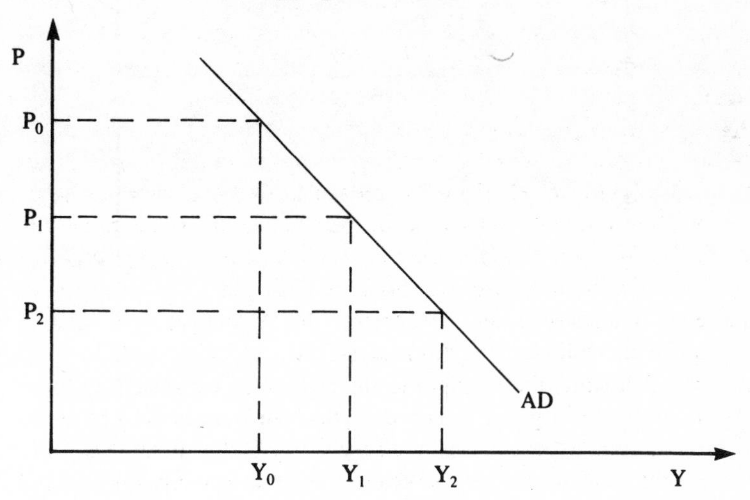

Figure 1.8 The 'classical' aggregate supply curve

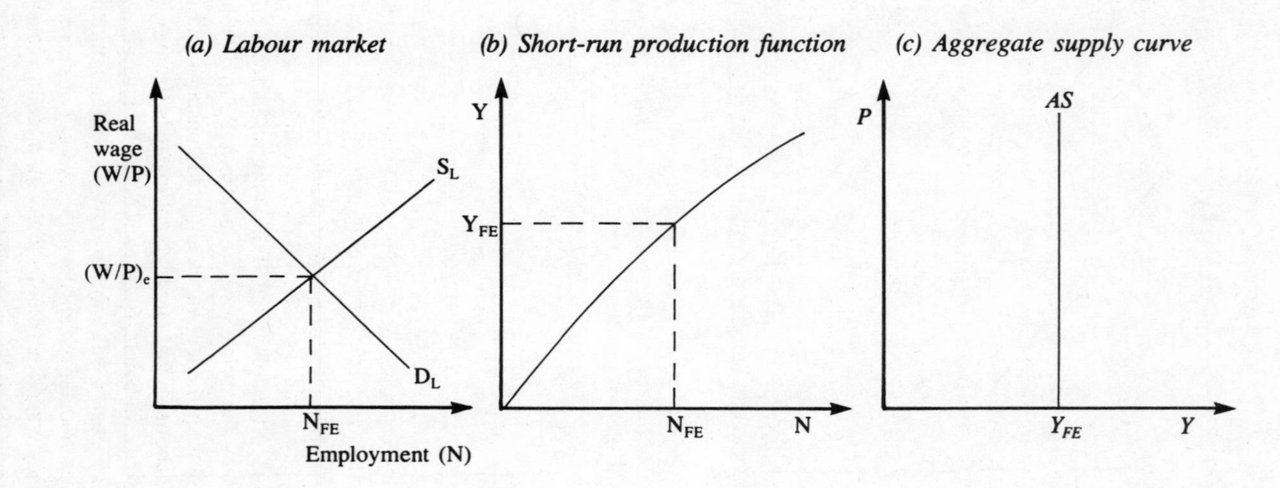

Having discussed the AD curve we now review the relationship between aggregate supply (AS) and the price level depicted in the AS curve.

The aggregate supply curve

The AS curve is derived from an analysis of the productive sector of the economy. If we consider the short-run production function in which the capital stock and technology are treated as being fixed, output varies with the input of the variable factor labour. The operation of the labour market within which the level of employment is determined is therefore fundamental in determining the output of the economy. In what follows we consider what effect different assumptions concerning the operation of the labour market have on the slope of the AS curve.

Let us begin with the classical assumption that both goods and labour markets are perfectly competitive. In this case the demand for labour varies inversely with the real wage (given a diminishing marginal product of labour) and the supply of labour varies positively with the real wage (assuming the substitution effect outweighs the income effect). The labour market clears at full employment equilibrium at a unique equilibrium level of the real wage (see Figure 1.8a). Where both labour demand and supply depend upon the real wage and the labour market clears then the level of employment and output (aggregate supply) will be invariant to the price level, resulting in a vertical AS curve (Figure 1.8c).

Let us now consider how the analysis is changed by introducing the traditional Keynesian assumption that the money wage is inflexible downwards and that workers suffer from money illusion. Assuming the money wage is not flexible downwards an excess supply of labour has no effect on the money (and real) wage and the labour market will fail to clear. For example, in Figure 1.9a for a given money wage and price level P_0 the labour market will fail to clear with employment at N_0. In the Keynesian approach the level of employment is determined by demand up to full employment. Following an increase in aggregate demand a rise in the price level (e.g. from P_0 to P_1) lowers the real wage (assuming money wages are held constant) and increases the demand for labour so that employment expands (from N_0 to N_1) resulting in an increase in output (i.e. from Y_0 to Y_1 in Figure 1.9b). The AS curve (see Figure 1.9c) will be upward sloping until full employment (Y_{FE}) is reached, at which point the AS curve becomes vertical (assuming money wages increase in line with price increases at full employment). In contrast to the assumption of an exogenous money wage which is

Figure 1.9 The 'Keynesian' aggregate supply curve

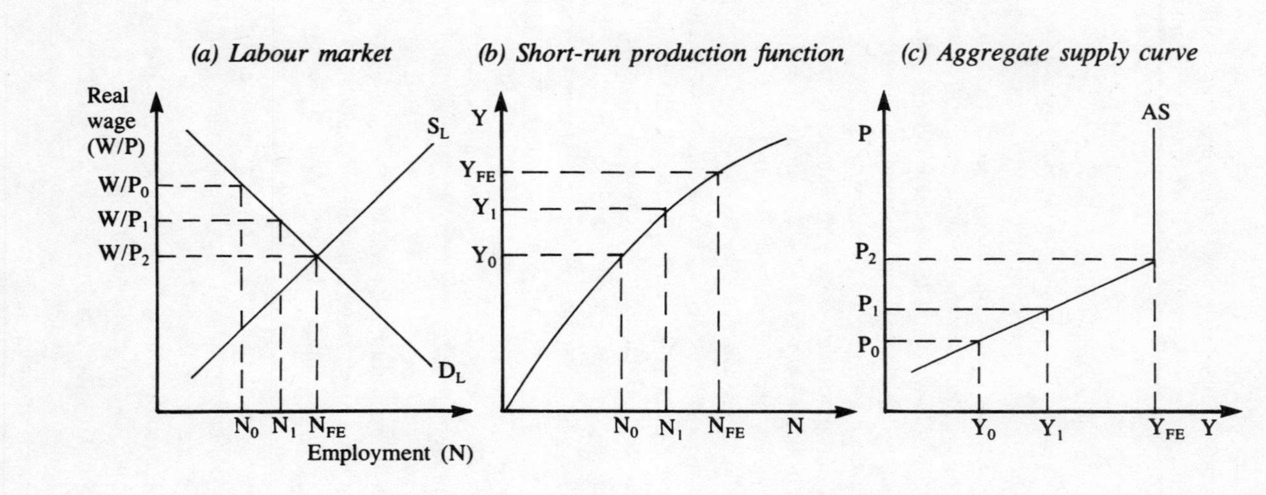

inflexible downwards underlying the traditional approach, modern Keynesian analysis accounts for the stickiness or inflexibility in the adjustment of money wages to prices due to (overlapping) wage contracts which fix wages for a specified time period. As in the traditional Keynesian approach, an increase in aggregate demand will be reflected in an increase in prices and output, producing a positively sloped aggregate supply curve at less than full employment (Figure 1.9c).

Finally in neoclassical analysis (monetarists and new classical economists) both labour demand and labour supply depend upon the real wage and in the long run the labour market clears at the equilibrium or natural rate of unemployment (see Chapter 3, section 3.4.2). In consequence the long-run aggregate supply curve is vertical at the natural rate of output and employment. At the natural rate of output and employment the price level is fully anticipated and the actual and expected price levels coincide. In the short run, however, actual unemployment

Figure 1.10 The 'neoclassical' aggregate supply curve

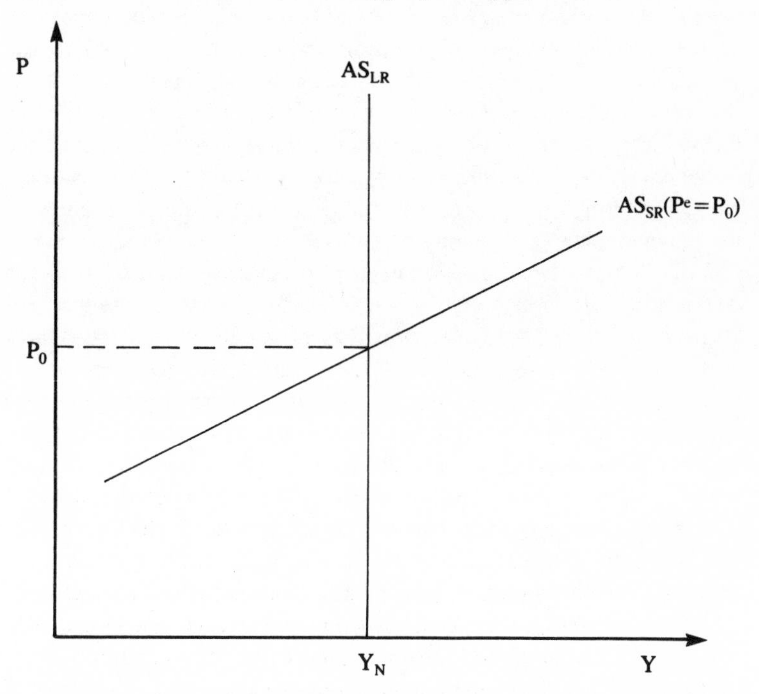

may be above or below the natural rate producing a positively sloped short-run aggregate supply curve. This is illustrated in Figure 1.10 where the short-run aggregate supply curve is drawn for a given expected price level and shows how output varies as the price level varies because agents act on price expectations which are incorrect. Central to this analysis is the role of incomplete information and the importance of price expectations in the process of adjustment.

In orthodox monetarist analysis the aggregate supply curve will be positively sloped in the short run when workers temporarily misperceive a change in real wages because they act on price expectations which are incorrect. Consider, for example, an economy which is initially in a position where output and employment are at their long-run equilibrium (natural) levels, i.e. a point where the short-run aggregate supply curve cuts the long-run aggregate supply curve where the price level is fully anticipated and the actual and expected price levels coincide. If aggregate demand increases, money wages and prices will increase as a result of excess demand in labour and goods markets. Workers, it is assumed, have imperfect knowledge of the general price level and only partially revise upwards their price expectations in line with the actual increase in prices. Workers then interpret the increase in money wages as an increase in real wages, and supply more labour. At the same time as the real wage falls firms (who it is assumed have knowledge of the price of the goods they sell and their wage costs) increase their demand for labour, resulting in an increase in employment and output. The only way to keep unemployment (output) below (above) the natural rate is to keep real wages below their equilibrium level by ensuring that product prices rise at a faster rate than money wages. Once workers realize that real wages have fallen, money wages will be raised until real wages return to their market clearing equilibrium level and output and employment return to their natural levels, i.e. a point on the long-run aggregate supply curve.

In new classical analysis output and employment will deviate from their long-run equilibrium (natural) levels (i.e. producing a positively sloped short-run aggregate supply curve) only in response to an unexpected change in the general price level. Errors in rationally formed price expectations (see the appendix to Chapter 3) it is assumed result from firms and workers having limited/incomplete information so that they mistake general price changes for relative price changes and react by changing the supply of output and labour. For example if aggregate demand increases, money wages and prices increase as a result of excess demand in labour and goods markets. Workers are assumed to have incomplete information and if they mistakenly perceive the increase in money wages as an increase in real wages they will respond by increasing the supply of labour. Firms are also assumed to have incomplete information in that they have information only on prices in the limited number of markets in which they trade. If individual firms mistake the increase in the price of their goods as an increase in the relative price of their output they will react by increasing their output. Workers and firms then are held to respond in the same direction to misperceived relative price increases by increasing the supply of labour and output respectively. Once agents realize that there has been no change in relative prices, output and employment return to their long-run equilibrium (natural) levels, i.e. a point on the long-run aggregate supply curve. The short-run supply curve is often called the 'surprise supply curve' and is examined in more detail in Chapter 6, section 6.4. In section 1.3.3 we examine more fully how only random and unanticipated shocks to aggregate demand cause errors in (rationally formed) price expectations

Figure 1.11 Keynesian approach: expansionary aggregate demand policies

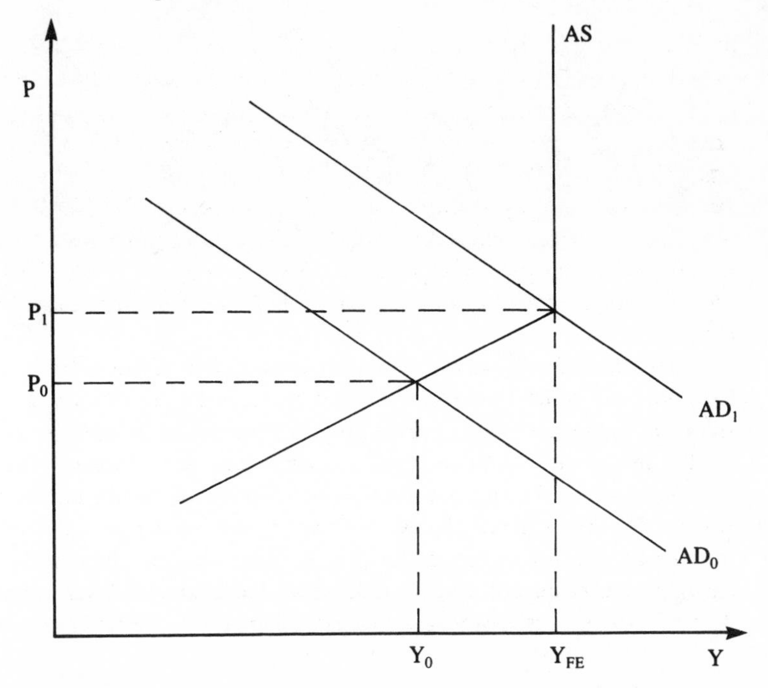

resulting in output and employment temporarily deviating from their long-run equilibrium (natural) levels.

The full AD-AS model

We are now in a position to place the AD and AS curves together and consider the effects of aggregate demand shocks on the economy. The equilibrium price level and equilibrium level of real output are determined where the AD and AS curves intersect. The policy implications that derive from this model critically depend on the slope of the AS schedule. In the Keynesian approach illustrated in Figure 1.11 expansionary aggregate demand policies result in both changes in the price level and real output up to full employment (Y_{FE}). For example, following an increase in aggregate demand from AD_0 to AD_1 income rises from Y_0 to Y_{FE} and the general price level increases from P_0 to P_1. After full employment is reached, further increases in aggregate demand result only in increases in the price level. In contrast in the neoclassical approach illustrated in

Figure 1.12 Neoclassical approach: expansionary aggregate demand policies

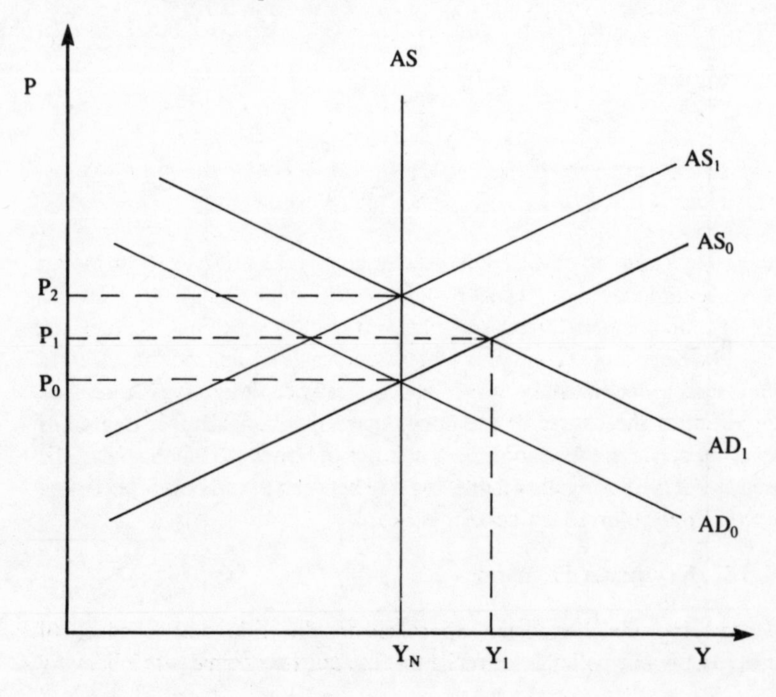

Figure 1.12, while expansionary aggregate demand policies affect both the price level and real output in the short run, in the long run they have no impact on the natural level of output and employment. In Figure 1.12 the economy is initially at P_0Y_N, i.e. the intersection of AD_0 AS_0 and AS. In the short run expansionary aggregate demand policies (AD_0 to AD_1) may cause an increase in the price level (from P_0 to P_1) and real output (from Y_N to Y_1). In the long run the increase in the price level causes the positively sloped short-run supply curve to shift upwards (from AS_0 to AS_1) until excess demand is eliminated and the economy returns to the natural level of output and employment (Y_N) with the price level at P_2. In section 1.3.3 we discuss more fully how monetarist and new classical economists differ in respect of the short-run impact effects on the economy of aggregate demand shocks.

1.3 MAINSTREAM SCHOOLS OF THOUGHT

Having revised the underlying structure and policy implications of the three most frequently employed textbook models of the macroeconomy we now turn to summarize the main areas of controversy between Keynesian, monetarist and new classical approaches over the role and conduct of macroeconomic stabilization policy, placing the major schools in the context of these textbook models. At the onset of this review it is important to stress that reference to these mainstream schools of thought, in this and subsequent chapters, is made purely for analytical convenience. The reader should bear in mind two points. First, there are differences of opinion and emphasis within each school. For example, there are a number of different and competing views on what constitutes the essential nature of Keynesian economics which include the Hicksian IS-LM model, the Clower-Leijonhufvud reinterpretation of Keynes and the new Keynesian economics with its emphasis on non-market clearing in the presence of sticky wages and prices. Secondly, as will become apparent in the course of the book, there is a considerable degree of overlap between the schools on a number of issues; so much so that the somewhat artificially drawn dividing line between the schools is becoming increasingly blurred on certain issues.

1.3.1 Keynesian Economics

Underlying the Keynesian approach to the role and conduct of macroeconomic policy is the belief that capitalist economies are inherently unstable and, if left to their own devices, can take a long time to return to the neighbourhood of full employment equilibrium after being subjected to some disturbance (due to sluggish adjustment of money wages and prices). Given the belief that the economy is not rapidly self-equilibrating, Keynesians stress the need for active interventionist policies and argue that the authorities can and consequently should use discretionary aggregate-demand management policies to stabilize the economy. Keynesians generally prefer to use discretionary fiscal policy as the main policy instrument as they consider the effects of fiscal policy on the level of aggregate demand to be more direct and predictable than those of monetary policy.

This Keynesian approach is usually associated with either the Keynesian cross or 45° line model, the IS-LM model or the Keynesian case of the AD-AS model. For example, in terms of the IS-LM model the Keynesian position has been characterized by a relatively flat LM curve and a relatively steep IS curve. In these circumstances disturbances from the real side of the economy (stochastic shifts in the IS curve) tend to dominate changes in income, and fiscal policy is preferred as the main policy instrument to maintain the economy at a high and stable level of employment. In short, in orthodox Keynesian analysis the aggregate level of output and employment is essentially determined by aggregate demand, though modern Keynesians also recognize the need for supply side as well as demand side policies to help stabilize the economy.

In order to explain inflation Keynesian economics has incorporated the expectations-augmented Phillips curve analysis (see Chapter 3, section 3.3). Most Keynesians tend to argue that the long-run Phillips curve is not vertical and that the government needs to, can and therefore should pursue an unemployment target via discretionary demand management policies. Such policies will involve inflation owing to the trade-off between unemployment and inflation but many Keynesians believe that the long-run Phillips curve can be shifted downward (i.e. achieving a lower rate of inflation at any given level of unemployment) by the adoption of a prices and incomes policy.

1.3.2 Monetarism

In contrast to Keynesian beliefs, monetarists argue that capitalist economies are inherently stable (unless disturbed by erratic monetary growth) and that when subjected to some disturbance the economy will return fairly rapidly to the neighbourhood of long-run equilibrium at the natural rate of unemployment. As such, they question the need for discretionary aggregate-demand management policies and tend to argue that such policies cannot and should not be used to stabilize the economy. While accepting that aggregate-demand policies can be used to influence the level of unemployment in the short run, they dispute the Keynesian view that the authorities can bring about a permanent reduction in the level of unemployment by macroeconomic policies involving the management of aggregate demand. Regarding fiscal policy monetarists argue that while pure fiscal expansion (i.e. without accommodating monetary expansion) can influence output and employment in the short run, in the long run it will have no effect on real income (see Chapter 5, section 5.3). Discretionary monetary policy can also influence output and employment in the short run but due to the length and variability of the time lags involved with monetary policy, monetarists argue that such policy could turn out to be destabilizing. Monetarists argue that if governments wish to reduce the natural rate of unemployment in order to achieve higher employment levels they should pursue microeconomic or what are referred to as supply side policies (e.g. designed to improve the structure of the labour market and the structure of industry) rather than macroeconomic policies.

The monetarist approach is usually associated with the neoclassical version of the AD-AS model as represented in Figure 1.12. Although the monetarist position is sometimes characterized in terms of the IS-LM model (i.e. by a relatively steep LM curve and a relatively flat IS curve) the static IS-LM model is inadequate as a frame of reference for monetarist analysis overall not least because it fails to: (i) incorporate a supply side to the model and (ii) accommodate simultaneous changes in prices and output and their interaction. The essence of the monetarist approach to the role and conduct of macroeconomic stabilization policy is better encapsulated in the neoclassical version of the AD-AS model in which aggregate-demand management policies only have real effects in the short run and with the economy tending to some natural rate of output and employment in the long run, i.e. a vertical long-run aggregate supply curve.

On the problem of inflation monetarists argue that inflation is essentially a monetary phenomenon propagated by excessive monetary growth. They accept that in the short run there may be a trade-off between inflation and unemployment but argue that once people have fully adjusted their inflationary expectations the trade-off disappears, resulting in a vertical long-run Phillips curve at the natural rate of unemployment. The belief in a vertical long-run Phillips curve implies that any attempt to maintain unemployment below the natural rate by discretionary demand management policies will result in accelerating inflation (see Chapter 3, section 3.4.3). Monetarists argue that if the authorities expand the money supply at a steady rate, over time the economy will tend to settle down at the natural rate of unemployment with a steady rate of inflation. In short, monetarists advocate that discretionary demand management policies should be replaced by a monetary rule in order to avoid economic instability.

1.3.3 New Classical Macroeconomics

The discussion so far has summarized the main elements of the Keynesian/monetarist debate over the role and conduct of macroeconomic stabilization policy. We now turn to outline the two most controversial policy implications that derive from the new classical approach to macroeconomics. At the onset it is important to stress that while new classical macroeconomics evolved out of monetarist macroeconomics during the 1970s and incorporates certain elements of monetarist macroeconomics (for example the monetary explanation of inflation) it can be argued that it is a separate school of thought from orthodox monetarism. In what follows we highlight the controversy between monetarists and new classical economists over: (i) whether aggregate demand policy changes announced by the authorities can influence output and employment in the short run, and (ii) the output/employment costs of reducing inflation.

As noted earlier, in monetarist analysis output and employment respond to an increase in aggregate demand in the short run whatever the nature of the increase in aggregate demand. In contrast new classical analysis predicts that announced aggregate demand policies will be ineffective in influencing the level of output and employment even in the short run and that only random and unanticipated shocks to aggregate demand will affect output and employment in the short run. This is illustrated in Figure 1.13. The economy is initially operating at P_0Y_N (i.e. the triple intersection of AD_0 AS_0 and AS), at which point the price level is fully anticipated and output is at its long-run equilibrium (natural) level.

Suppose the authorities announce that they intend to increase the money supply. Rational economic agents would take this information into account in forming their expectations and fully anticipate the effects of the increase in the money supply on the general price level so that output and employment would remain unchanged at the long-run equilibrium

Figure 1.13 Neoclassical approach: the effects of anticipated and unanticipated changes in aggregate demand

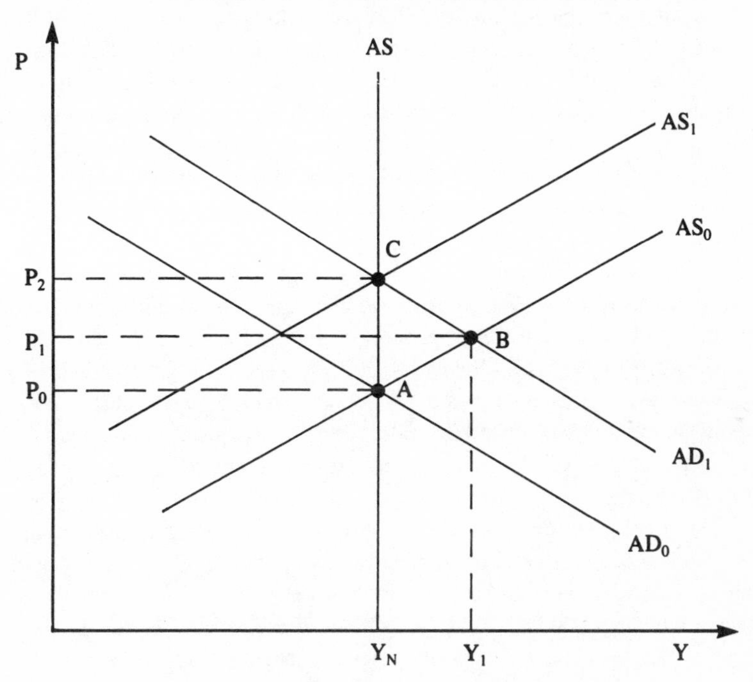

(natural) levels. The rightward shift of the AD curve from AD_0 to AD_1 would be offset by an upward shift to the left of the positively sloped AS curve (from AS_0 to AS_1) following an immediate revision of price expectations. In this case the economy would move straight from point A to C, remaining on the vertical long-run aggregate supply curve with no change in output and employment even in the short run. This adjustment process then corresponds to the monetarist case in the long run and the new classical case in the short run provided that the aggregate demand policy changes are anticipated.

Suppose now that the authorities surprise economic agents by increasing the money supply without announcing their intentions. In this situation workers/firms with limited information would mistakenly perceive this as a real (as opposed to a nominal) increase in demand for their services/goods and respond by increasing the supply of labour/output. In other words, firms and workers would misperceive the resulting increase in the general price level as an increase in relative prices and react by increasing the supply of output and labour. In terms of Figure 1.13 the aggregate demand curve would shift to the right from AD_0 to AD_1 and intersect the positively sloped aggregate supply curve AS_0 at P_1Y_1, i.e. the economy would move from point A to B. The increase in output and employment would, however, only be temporary. Once agents realized that there had been no change in relative prices, output and employment would quickly return to their long-run equilibrium (natural) levels. In terms of Figure 1.13, as economic agents fully adjusted their price expectations the positively sloped aggregate supply curve would shift upwards from AS_0 to AS_1 and the economy would move from point B to C. This adjustment process corresponds to the monetarist case in the short run whatever the nature of the increase in aggregate demand, and the new classical case in the short run when the aggregate demand policy changes are unanticipated. However, adjustment in the new classical case would be much quicker than that envisaged by orthodox monetarists.

The strong policy conclusion – that anticipated aggregate demand policies will be ineffective in influencing the level of output and employment even in the short run, and that only random and unanticipated shocks to aggregate demand (such as an unanticipated increase in the money supply) can temporarily affect output and employment – has profound implications for the role and conduct of macroeconomic stabilization policy. If, for example, the money supply is determined by the authorities according to some known rule, the authorities will be unable to influence output and employment even in the short run by pursuing a systematic monetary policy. Only departures from this rule (i.e. errors by the monetary authorities or unforeseen changes in policy) can influence real output. Any attempt to affect output and employment by random or non-systematic aggregate demand policies would, it is argued, only increase the variation of output and employment around their natural levels. The new classical approach provides a distinct and potentially more damaging reason to the reasons put forward by orthodox monetarists, to question whether traditional stabilization policies can be used to improve the performance of the economy. Having said this, it is important to note that the policy ineffectiveness result derives from the structure of new classical models and in particular the assumption of continuous market clearing. Keynesian-like disequilibrium models (i.e. where markets do not clear continuously due to sluggish price adjustment) which incorporate rational expectations still allow a role for demand management policies to stabilize the economy at the natural level of output and employment. This is illustrated in Figure 1.14.

Figure 1.14 New-Keynesian approach: the effects of unanticipated changes in aggregate demand

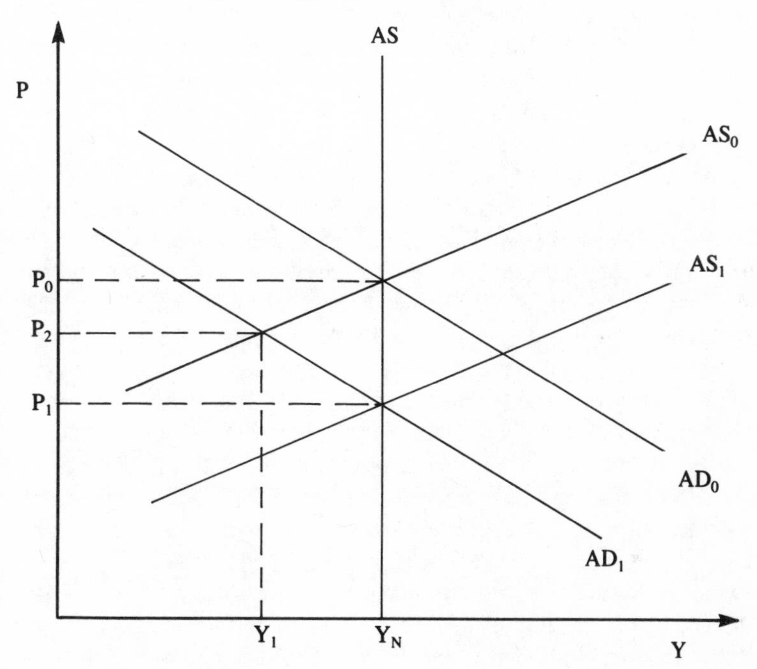

In Figure 1.14 the economy is initially operating at the triple intersection of AS, AD_0 and AS_0 at which point the price level (P_0) is fully anticipated and output is at its long-run equilibrium level (Y_N). Following a sudden and unexpected decrease in aggregate demand the aggregate demand curve would shift downwards to the left from AD_0 to AD_1 resulting in a fall in the price level from P_0 to P_2 and output from Y_N to Y_1. In order to restore labour market clearing, money wages would have to be renegotiated to a lower level such that the short-run aggregate supply curve shifted downward from AS_0 to AS_1 reducing the price level to P_1 and restoring output to Y_N. If, in the face of random shocks to aggregate demand, the government is able to adjust its policies more quickly than the private sector can renegotiate money wages there is still a role for aggregate demand management to stabilize the economy and offset fluctuations in output and employment around their natural levels.

The second main area of policy controversy between monetarists and new classical economists concerns the output/employment costs of reducing inflation. New classical macroeconomics incorporates the monetarist view that inflation: (i) is essentially a monetary phenomenon propagated by excessive monetary growth, and (ii) can only be reduced by slowing down the rate of monetary expansion. However, new classical economists and orthodox monetarists disagree on the output/employment costs of reducing inflation. Orthodox monetarists predict that unemployment will rise following monetary contraction, the extent and duration of which depends on the degree of monetary contraction and how quickly people adjust downward their expectations of future rates of inflation (see Chapter 3, section 3.4.4). In contrast the new classical approach suggests that an announced and believed reduction in the rate of monetary expansion will have little or no effect on the level of output and employment even in the short run. In their view, rational economic agents would quickly adjust their expectations of inflation in a downward direction according to the anticipated effects of the announced monetary contraction so that any fall in output and employment would be small and temporary, i.e. the downward shift of the short-run Phillips curve would be almost immediate. In consequence there is no necessity to follow the policy prescription of gradual monetary contraction advocated by orthodox monetarists. Given the absence of output/employment costs the authorities might just as well announce a dramatic reduction in the rate of monetary expansion in order to reduce inflation to their preferred target rate.

Having summarized the main areas of controversy between Keynesian, monetarist and new classical approaches over the role and conduct of macroeconomic stabilization policy we are now in a position to begin our more detailed examination of selected key issues in macroeconomics. We begin with a discussion of the role the external environment plays in influencing the domestic fiscal and monetary policy pursued in an open economy.

2. The Balance of Payments and Exchange Rates

2.1 INTRODUCTION

The purpose of this chapter is to outline the links between the external environment and domestic economic activity, in particular the balance of payments and/or the exchange rate, and the restraints imposed on domestic fiscal and monetary policy in an open economy. Of fundamental importance to such a discussion is the type of exchange rate regime in existence. Up to the abandonment of the Bretton Woods system in the early 1970s the major industrial countries operated under a regime of fixed exchange rates. Under a system of fixed exchange rates it is essential to consider how far the balance of payments imposes a constraint on macroeconomic policy. With the advent of floating/flexible exchange rates in the early 1970s (1972 in the case of the UK) it has become necessary to consider the importance of the behaviour of the exchange rate to macroeconomic policy. Under a system of freely (pure or clean) floating/flexible exchange rates the exchange rate adjusts to clear the foreign exchange market (that is, the central monetary authorities do not intervene in the market to influence the exchange rate) so that the sum of the current and capital accounts of the balance of payments is always zero. However since 1972–3 a situation somewhere between fixed and pure floating exchange rates has prevailed. The exchange rate regime has in fact been one of managed or dirty floating exchange rates where governments have frequently intervened, in varying degrees, in foreign exchange markets to influence exchange rates. In contrast to pure floating exchange rates the overall balance of payments does not sum to zero under a regime of dirty floating exchange rates. Bearing this in mind the layout of the chapter is as follows. In sections 2.2 and 2.3 we discuss the different insights offered by the Keynesian and monetary approaches to the balance of payments into the extent to which the balance of payments imposes a constraint on macroeconomic policy. In sections 2.4 and 2.5 we examine the Keynesian and monetary approaches to macroeconomic policy and the behaviour of the exchange rate under a system of flexible exchange rates. Finally in section 2.6 we consider exchange rate models which provide somewhat different insights into the analysis of exchange rate adjustment and allow for the possibility of exchange rate overshooting.

2.2 THE MUNDELL–FLEMING: KEYNESIAN MODEL UNDER FIXED EXCHANGE RATES

The Keynesian approach to balance of payments policy can best be analysed using a model first developed by Mundell and Fleming at the start of the 1960s (see Mundell 1962, 1963 and Fleming 1962). Early Keynesian analysis of the balance of payments focused on the determination of the current account and how government policy could improve the balance of payments on the current account (in particular the conditions under which devaluation would be successful in doing just this). Ignoring capital flows in the 1940s and early 1950s was understandable given that at that time private capital flows were of minimal significance (due to exchange controls). The late 1950s/early 1960s, however, witnessed a period of increasingly liberalized trade and capital movements and against this background Mundell and Fleming extended the Keynesian model of an open economy to include capital flows.

2.2.1 The Overall Balance of Payments and the BP Curve

In order to set out the complete Mundell–Fleming model we need briefly to discuss the determination of the current and capital accounts. At the onset of this discussion it is important to note that we make two simplifying assumptions. First, we assume given levels of the world income, interest rate and price level; the exchange rate; and the domestic price level. Secondly, we assume that we are dealing with a small open country in the sense that changes within the domestic economy of that country and its macroeconomic policies have an insignificant effect on the rest of the world economy.

Let us begin with the determination of the current account. Within the standard fixed-price Keynesian model of an open economy imports are a function of domestic income and relative prices (of domestic and foreign goods) while exports are a function of world income and relative prices.

Ceteris paribus, as domestic income rises imports increase (i.e. the marginal propensity to import is greater than zero) and the balance of payments on the current account worsens. We now turn to the capital account. As noted earlier, Mundell and Fleming extended this Keynesian model to include capital flows postulating that, with static expectations about exchange rate changes, net capital flows are a function of the differential between domestic and foreign interest rates. *Ceteris paribus*, as the domestic interest rate rises domestic assets become more attractive and the capital account of the balance of payments improves due to the resulting inward flow of funds.

The overall balance of payments is the sum of the current and capital accounts and this analysis can be shown graphically within the familiar IS-LM framework. The BP curve (see Figure 2.1) depicts a locus of combinations of domestic interest rates and income levels that yield an overall zero balance of payments position on the combined current and capital accounts. The BP curve is positively sloped because if balance of payments equilibrium is to be maintained (i.e. a zero overall balance)

Figure 2.1 The Mundell–Fleming/Keynesian model

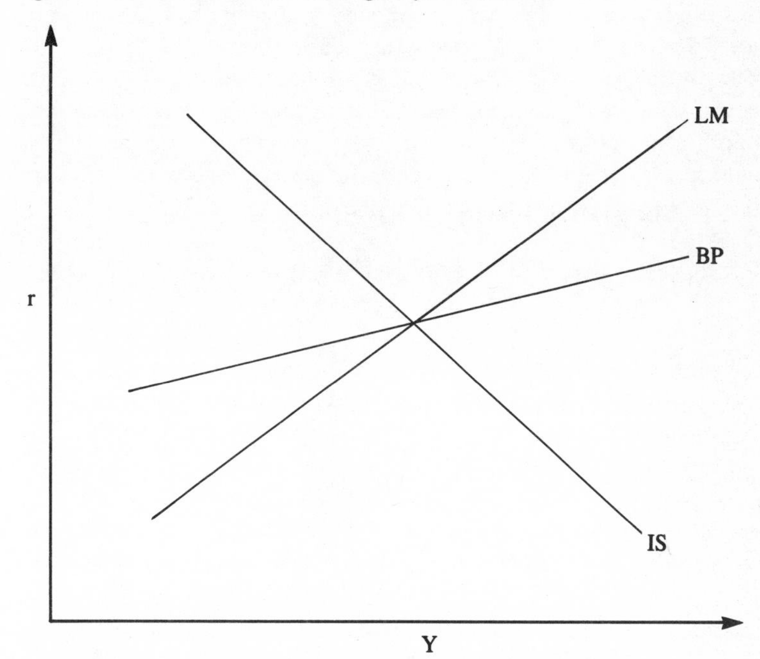

then increases (decreases) in the level of domestic income which worsen (improve) the current account have to be accompanied by increases (decreases) in the domestic rate of interest which improve (worsen) the capital account. Points above and to the left of the BP curve are associated with an overall balance of payments surplus, while points below and to the right of the BP curve indicate an overall balance of payments deficit. Given the level of income a point above (below) the BP curve generates an overall payments surplus (deficit) since the domestic rate of interest is higher (lower) than that necessary to produce an overall zero balance of payments position. The slope of the BP curve depends on the marginal propensity to import and the interest elasticity of international capital flows. Other things being equal, the smaller (larger) is the marginal propensity to import and the more (less) interest elastic are capital flows, the flatter (steeper) the slope of the BP curve will be. With respect to the interest elasticity of international capital movements it is interesting to note that in the two limiting cases of perfect capital mobility and complete capital immobility the BP curve would become horizontal and vertical respectively.

Equilibrium in the goods (IS curve) and money markets (LM curve) and in the balance of payments (BP curve) requires the intersection of all three lines at the same point. This is also illustrated in Figure 2.1. The crucial policy issue facing the authorities is to seek to ensure that at this point both internal (output and employment) and external (balance of payments) objectives are met. Before discussing this problem we first need to analyse the effect of a change in fiscal and monetary policy on the balance of payments within the model.

2.2.2 The Effect of a Change in Fiscal and Monetary Policy on Income and the Balance of Payments

Under a regime of fixed exchange rates expansionary fiscal policy may lead to either an improvement or a deterioration in the overall balance of payments position, and vice versa for a contractionary policy. This is illustrated in the two panels of Figure 2.2. In Figure 2.2a the LM curve is steeper than the BP curve, while in Figure 2.2b the converse is true. In both panels of Figure 2.2 the economy is initially at point A, the triple intersection of the curves IS_0 LM and BP with equilibrium in the goods and money markets, and in the balance of payments. Expansionary fiscal policy shifts the IS curve from IS_0 to IS_1 and results in an increase in the domestic rate of interest from r_0 to r_1 (improving

Figure 2.2 Fiscal expansion under imperfect capital mobility

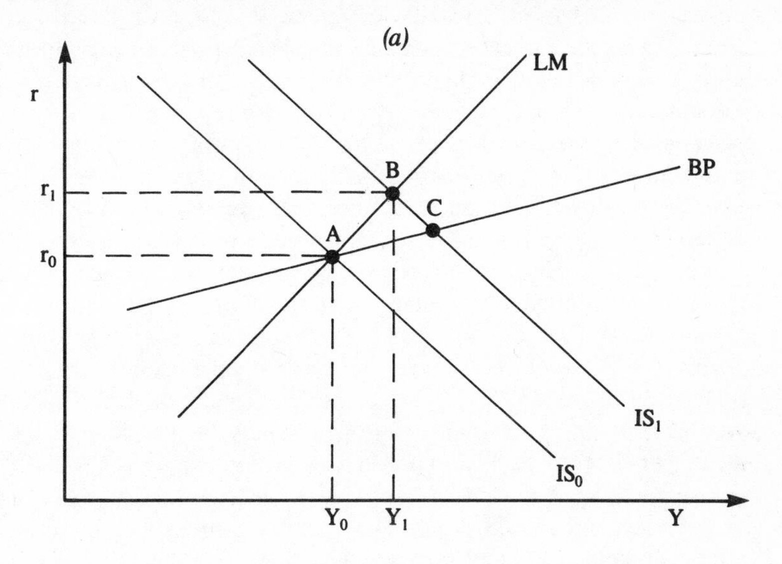

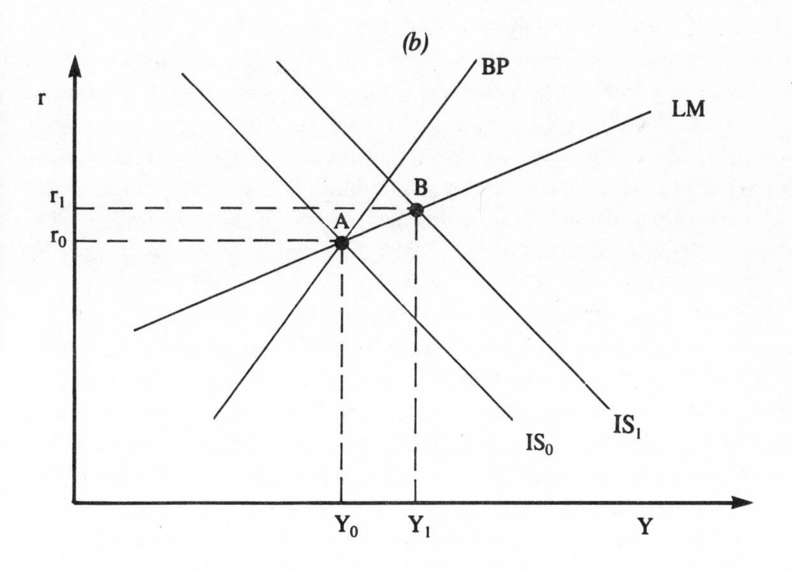

the capital account) and an increase in income from Y_0 to Y_1 (worsening the current account). As can be seen from panels (a) and (b) of Figure 2.2 the net outcome on the overall balance of payments position depends on the relative slopes of the LM and BP curves (i.e. the structural parameters underlying the model). In Figure 2.2a the net outcome is an overall balance of payments surplus at point B. (i.e. IS_1 and LM intersect at a point above the BP curve), while in Figure 2.2b it is one of an overall deficit (i.e. IS_1 and LM intersect at point B below the BP curve). Expansionary fiscal policy is more likely to lead to an improvement in the overall balance of payments position: (i) the smaller is the marginal propensity to import and the more interest elastic are capital flows (i.e. the flatter the slope of the BP curve is) and (ii) the greater is the income elasticity and the smaller is the interest elasticity of the demand for money (i.e. the steeper the slope of the LM is), and vice versa. In practice it is likely that the LM curve will be steeper than the BP curve due to the interest elasticity of the demand for money being less than that for capital flows. This view tends to be backed up by the available empirical evidence and will be adopted in the following discussion concerning long-run equilibrium.

One crucial point worth noting is that in analysing the consequences for the balance of payments of domestic fiscal policy under fixed exchange rates the Keynesian approach assumes that the authorities can sterilize the effects of a balance of payments surplus or deficit on the money stock in the short run (providing there is imperfect capital mobility). In the long run it becomes increasingly difficult to sterilize the effects of a persistent surplus or deficit on the money stock so that the results analysed above necessarily relate to the short run.

Long-run equilibrium requires a zero balance on the balance of payments otherwise the domestic money supply changes in the manner discussed in section 2.3. More particularly the balance of payments surplus implicit at point B in Figure 2.2a will cause an expansion of the domestic money supply following intervention by the authorities to maintain the fixed exchange rate. This causes the LM curve to shift outwards and the long-run equilibrium will occur at point C where the balance of payments is zero and the real and monetary sectors are in equilibrium.

In contrast, expansionary monetary policy will always lead to a deterioration in the balance of payments, and vice versa. This is illustrated in Figure 2.3. The economy is initially at point A, the intersection of the three curves IS, LM_0 and BP with equilibrium in the goods and money markets, and in the balance of payments. Expansionary monetary policy shifts the LM curve from LM_0 to LM_1 and results in a reduction in the domestic rate of interest from r_0 to r_1 (worsening the capital account) and an increase in the level of income from Y_0 to Y_1 (worsening the current account). With adverse interest and income effects on the capital and current accounts respectively, the overall balance of payments is unambiguously in deficit at point B (i.e. IS and LM_1 intersect at a point below the BP curve). The reader should verify for himself/herself that in the case where the BP curve is steeper than the LM curve expansionary (contractionary) monetary policy will still lead to a deterioration (improvement) in the balance of payments.

Figure 2.3 Monetary expansion under imperfect capital mobility

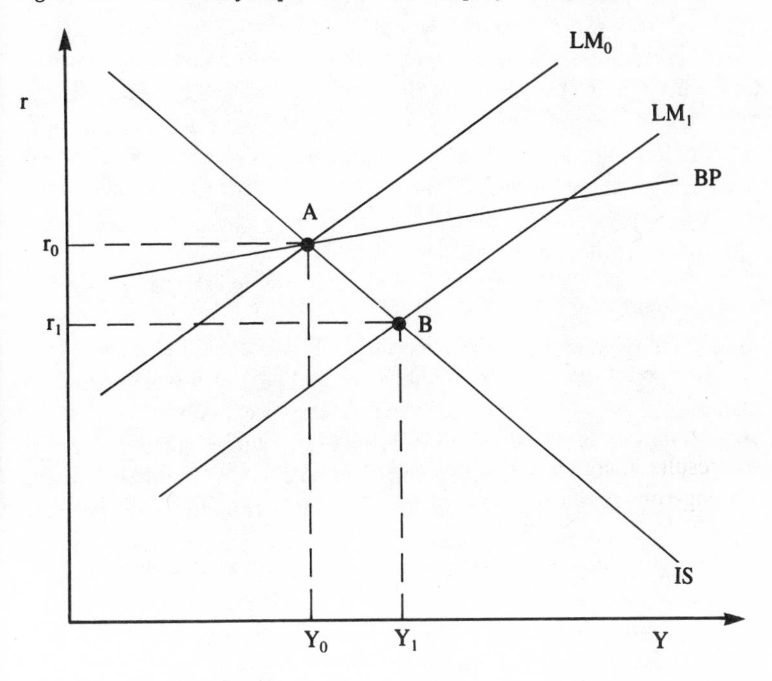

In a similar manner to that discussed for fiscal policy, point B cannot be a long-run equilibrium. The implied balance of payments deficit causes a contraction in the money supply shifting the LM curve backwards. The long-run adjustment process will cease at point A where the LM curve has returned to its original position. In other words, in the absence of sterilization, monetary policy is completely ineffective as far as influencing real income is concerned. This assumes that the domestic country is small relative to the rest of the world so that the expansion of its money supply has a negligible effect on the world money supply – see section 2.3.3 for further discussion of this point.

2.2.3 The Assignment Problem

We are now in a position to discuss the central policy issue referred to as the assignment problem. Equilibrium for the economic system as a whole requires that the IS, LM and BP curves all intersect at the same point. The problem facing the authorities is successfully to secure the twin objectives of internal (output and employment at their full employment levels) and external (a zero overall balance of payments position) balance by the appropriate mix of fiscal and monetary policy. Mundell's solution requires the correct assignment of each policy instrument to the objective on which it has the most influence and involves the assignment of monetary policy to attain balance of payment adjustment and fiscal policy to attain output and employment objectives. This is illustrated in the two panels of Figure 2.4.

In Figure 2.4a the economy is initially operating at point A, the triple intersection of IS_0 LM_0 and BP with external balance (a zero overall balance of payments position) and internal imbalance (i.e. income level Y_0 is below its full employment level Y_F). In this situation the appropriate policy mix involves expansionary fiscal policy to secure full employment and expansionary monetary policy to maintain balance of payments equilibrium. Internal and external balance would be achieved at point B, the intersection of the three curves IS_1 LM_1 and BP. The reader should verify for himself/herself that in the initial situation illustrated in Figure 2.4a but with the BP curve steeper than the LM curve the appropriate policy mix would involve expansionary fiscal policy to secure full employment and contractionary monetary policy to maintain balance of payments equilibrium.

Consider another example. In Figure 2.4b the economy is initially at point A with income at full employment (internal balance) and a balance of payments deficit (external imbalance) as IS_0 and LM_0 intersect at a point below the BP curve. In this situation the appropriate policy mix involves contractionary monetary policy to secure balance of payments equilibrium and expansionary fiscal policy to maintain output at its full employment level. Internal and external balance would be achieved at

Figure 2.4

(a) External balance/internal imbalance

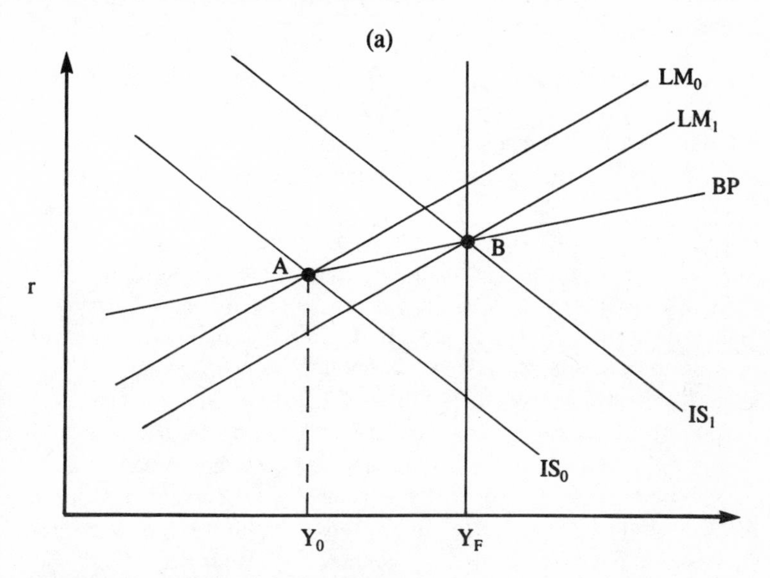

(b) Internal balance/external imbalance

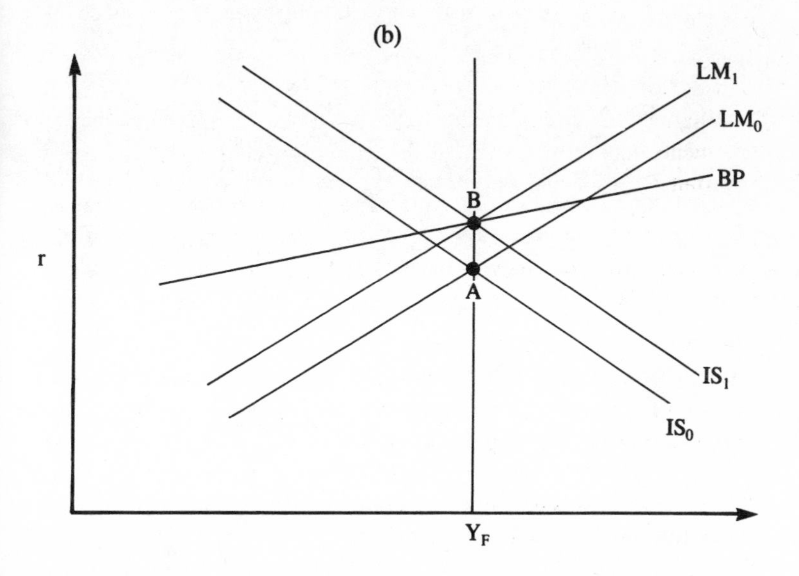

point B, the triple intersection of IS_1 LM_1 and BP. Note that in this analysis we have abstracted from the practical difficulties of implementing the precise mix of fiscal and monetary policy necessary to achieve the desired objectives.

2.2.4 Concluding Comments

The model we have been discussing provides some useful insights into the problem of simultaneously attaining internal and external balance solely by way of the appropriate mix and correct assignment of monetary and fiscal policy (i.e. without recourse to such expenditure-switching policies as devaluation or import controls). The reader should be aware, however, that this approach to balance of payments policy has been subjected to a number of criticisms. Brief mention of two of the main criticisms will suffice. First, within the model net capital flows between countries depend on the differential between domestic and foreign interest rates. This specification of the capital account can be questioned on the grounds that it is inconsistent with portfolio theory, which suggests that perpetual capital flows require continuous interest rate changes (i.e. a continuous change in the domestic interest rate relative to foreign interest rates). Secondly, the model implicitly assumes that a country is able to match a continuous deficit on the current account by a surplus on the capital account. Yet there is a number of reasons why this assumption can be questioned and why, in consequence, the nature of the balance of payments objective is likely to be much more precise than just overall balance of payments equilibrium. For example, the credit-worthiness of a country running a persistent current account deficit may be brought into doubt to such an extent that it can only secure the necessary capital account surplus for an overall zero balance of payments position by progressively raising its domestic interest rate. In the long run it is much more likely that a country will need to achieve a balance on the current account. We now turn to discuss the monetary approach to the balance of payments.

2.3 THE MONETARY APPROACH TO THE BALANCE OF PAYMENTS UNDER FIXED EXCHANGE RATES

2.3.1 Balance of Payments: a Monetary Phenomenon

The late 1960s and early 1970s witnessed a number of important contributions to the development of the monetary approach to the balance of payments (see Frenkel and Johnson 1976). Within the monetary approach the balance of payments is treated as essentially a monetary phenomenon in which the relationship between the stock demand for and supply of money is regarded as the main determinant of balance of payments flows. This does not mean that real (i.e. non-monetary) factors do not influence the balance of payments but rather that their impact is examined through the effect they have on the demand for and supply of money balances. Any discrepancy between actual and desired money balances results in balance of payments deficits/surpluses (the overall net balance on the current and capital accounts), which in turn provide the mechanism whereby the discrepancy is eliminated. Under fixed exchange rates, a balance of payments surplus can be the result of either an excess demand for money by domestic units, or an excess supply of money created abroad. Conversely, a deficit can be the result of either an excess supply of money created by the domestic monetary authority (i.e. excessive domestic credit expansion) or an excess demand for money from abroad.

2.3.2 Monetary models

While a number of monetary models with different specifications have appeared in the literature, the following key assumptions are usually made:

1. Both the demand for and supply of money are stable functions of a limited number of variables.
2. Long-run equilibrium in a macroeconomic model requires both stock and flow equilibrium in all markets.
3. In the long run, changes in the money supply arising out of balance of payments deficits/surpluses cannot be neutralized i.e. the authorities cannot sterilize balance of payments deficits/surpluses for any significant period of time.
4. In the long run, income tends towards its full employment or natural level, a level determined mainly by real factors independently of monetary policy; and
5. In the absence of trade barriers, and after allowing for transport costs, perfect commodity arbitrage will ensure that the law of one price must hold for similar traded goods.

Following Johnson (1972), one of the most influential contributors to the literature on the monetary approach, we consider a simple monetary model of the balance of payments in which: (i) real income is fixed at its full employment or natural level; (ii) the law of one price holds in goods and asset markets and (iii) we deal with a small open economy whose price level and interest rate are pegged to world levels. Given these assumptions, domestic income, prices and interest rates are all given exogenously. The real demand for money depends on real income and the rate of interest (equation 2.1) while the supply of money is equal to money created domestically (domestic credit) plus money associated with changes in international reserves (equation 2.2).

$$Md = P\, f(y, r) \tag{2.1}$$

$$Ms = D + R \tag{2.2}$$

If the system is initially in equilibrium the demand for money will equal the supply of money and there will be no changes in international reserves.

We now examine the consequences of a once and for all increase in domestic credit (D) by the authorities. With real income fixed at its full employment or natural level and the domestic price level and interest rate tied to world levels (by the law of one price) the arguments in the demand for money function are exogenously given. In other words the demand for money cannot adjust to the increase in the supply of money. Individuals will dispose of their excess money balances by purchasing foreign goods and securities, generating a balance of payments deficit and an associated loss of international reserves. The process will continue until actual and desired real balances are brought back into balance. The system will return to equilibrium when the money supply returns to its original level (i.e. adjustment is via the money supply rather than the demand for money) with the increase in domestic credit being offset by a fall in the country's international reserves – in equation (2.2) the fall in R exactly matches the rise in D so that Ms remains constant.

The analysis can also be conducted in dynamic terms. Consider, for example, an economy experiencing continuous real income growth with constant prices and interest rates. The balance of payments position reflects the relationship between the growth of domestic credit and the growth of money demand. If the authorities fail to expand domestic credit in line with the growth in the demand for money balances (due to real income growth) then the country will experience a persistent balance of payments surplus and will be continually acquiring international reserves. Persistent surpluses (deficits) can only occur if the domestic monetary authority allows domestic credit to expand less (more) than the public wants to expand its money holdings. In the short run a country might aim to expand domestic credit below the expected growth in money demand in order to achieve a balance of payments surplus and build up depleted international reserves. In the long run, however, it would be irrational for a country to pursue a policy of achieving continuous balance of payments surpluses since, in reality, it would mean that the country was willing to trade without limit goods for international reserves (conversely the level of foreign exchange reserves provides a limit to the duration of time a country could finance an ongoing balance of payments deficit). At the same time, given that the monetary approach also provides an automatic adjustment mechanism to correct external imbalance there is no reason why a country should want to continuously build up its international reserves. It is to this automatic adjustment mechanism to the balance of payments and the other main policy implications of the approach that we now turn.

2.3.3 Policy Implications of the Monetary Approach

Automatic adjustment mechanism

The monetary approach provides an automatic adjustment mechanism that operates without discretionary policy to correct balance of payments disequilibria. As we have seen, money market disequilibrium (discrepancy between actual and desired real money balances) will cause flow disequilibrium in the balance of payments as people try to get rid of or acquire real money balances through international markets for goods and securities. This adjustment process will continue until such time as the source of the disturbance has ceased, in other words, when real balances are back to their desired level so that in the long run there is full stock equilibrium and the overall balance of payments has a zero net balance.

Power of expenditure-switching policies

Closely linked to the existence of a monetary mechanism that ensures the automatic adjustment of balance of payments disequilibria is the prediction, that, by themselves, expenditure-switching policies will fail to produce any lasting improvement in the balance of payments. In this context devaluation would raise the domestic price level (via the law of one price) and hence lower the level of real balances below their equilibrium level, causing domestic residents to attempt to restore their real balances through international commodity and security markets. If there was no domestic credit expansion the excess demand for money would generate a balance of payments surplus, which in turn would remove the excess demand by increasing the level of foreign exchange reserves. The monetary approach also implies that import quotas, tariffs, exchange controls and other restrictions on trade and payments will improve the balance of payments only if they induce an increase in the demand for money by raising domestic prices. However, like devaluation, the effects will be transitory and will continue only until the stock of money is increased through balance of payments surpluses to meet the increased demand.

Power of monetary policy

The last prediction of the monetary approach we shall examine concerns the power of monetary policy. In the case of a small country relative to the rest of the world the country's money supply becomes an endogenous rather than a policy variable. Domestic monetary policy only determines the division of the country's money supply between domestic credit and foreign exchange reserves (see equation 2.2). Monetary policy controls the volume of domestic credit (the money supply being endogenous) which in turn influences the balance of payments and hence the foreign exchange reserves of the country. For example, given the assumption of full employment and the law of one price, we have seen that if the domestic monetary authority allows domestic credit to expand faster than the public wants to expand its money holdings, the public will get rid of these additional balances by increasing their expenditure on foreign goods and securities. This will generate a balance of payments deficit and lead to a reduction in the international reserves backing the domestic money supply. In this situation the rate of change of foreign exchange reserves (the balance of payments) varies to eliminate any discrepancy between the rate of domestic credit expansion and the rate of change of the demand for money. In the case of a small country, then, monetary policy is completely impotent to influence any variable (other than foreign exchange reserves) in the long run, since an increase in domestic credit will be matched by an equal reduction in foreign exchange reserves (through the balance of payments deficit) with no effect on the money supply. In the absence of the small-country assumption, monetary policy will have some effect depending upon a country's size relative to the rest of the world. The larger the proportionate size of the country, the greater will be the effect of domestic monetary policy; this is particularly relevant to the United States, whose size and importance in the world economy provides some scope for monetary policy to be effective.

2.3.4 Concluding comments

The monetary approach to the balance of payments has been subjected to a number of criticisms and in what follows we will briefly mention three of these. The first concerns the law of one price which is assumed in many models of the monetary approach to the balance of payments (e.g. the model used in section 2.3.2). While it is apparent that the law is of dubious validity, especially in the short run, adherents of the approach argue that this assumption is used only as a simplification to facilitate the exposition of the model and is not essential to the analysis. What is essential is that after due allowance for tariffs and transport costs prices of similar traded goods will tend to be equalized in the long run. A second more important potential source of criticism is whether governments can and do neutralize the monetary impact of balance of payments surpluses/deficits on the domestic money supply. Empirical evidence on neutralization showing a range of experience is far from clear and suggests that some countries have been able to sterilize, at least partially, the effects of the balance of payments on the domestic money supply and have been able to run balance of payments surpluses or deficits for quite long periods without the automatic adjustment mechanism working. The final criticism we note is that it has been argued that the monetary approach with its concentration on the long run renders the analysis useless in so far as policy measures towards the balance of payments are determined in a short-run environment.

From the discussion of sections 2.2 and 2.3 it will be apparent that due to the different assumptions underlying the two models (the Mundell–Fleming/Keynesian model and the monetary model), Keynesians and monetarists differ in their approaches to balance of payments policy. One of the essential differences is that the Keynesian (less than full employment) model is concerned with the short run, when it is assumed the authorities can sterilize balance of payments surpluses and deficits, while the monetary (full employment) model is a long-run model in which sterilization does not occur.

We now turn to discuss macroeconomic policy and the behaviour of the exchange rate under a system of freely (pure or clean) floating/flexible exchange rates. Under such a system the exchange rate adjusts to clear the foreign exchange market so that the sum of the current and capital accounts of the balance of payments is always zero, that is the central monetary authorities do not intervene in the foreign exchange market to influence the exchange rate. The analysis is essentially the same as that discussed earlier for fixed exchange rates. The only difference is that the balance of payments is assumed to be zero and the exchange rate fluctuates. In essence the difference is between a model where prices are assumed to be fixed and quantities vary, and where the quantity is fixed (balance of payments zero) and the price (the exchange rate) varies. We begin with a discussion of the Keynesian approach using the Mundell–Fleming model outlined in section 2.2.1.

2.4 THE MUNDELL–FLEMING: KEYNESIAN MODEL UNDER FLEXIBLE EXCHANGE RATES

At the onset of our discussion of the Keynesian model it is important to note that we again make the following two simplifying assumptions. First, we assume that the world income and interest rate are given exogenously. Secondly, we assume that we are dealing with a small open economy relative to the rest of the world.

We begin with a brief recap of the determination of the current and capital accounts of the balance of payments. Within the standard fixed-price Keynesian model of an open economy imports are a function of domestic income and relative prices (of domestic and foreign goods), while exports are a function of world income and relative prices. Relative prices will change following a change in the exchange rate. A depreciation of the domestic currency will lower the price of domestic goods relative to foreign goods (when both prices are expressed in the same currency), resulting in a shift in demand from foreign to domestic goods, and vice versa. *Ceteris paribus*, net exports will increase (i.e. the current account will improve) as the exchange rate depreciates, provided the Marshall–Lerner conditions are fulfilled. These conditions require that starting from an initially balanced trade position and assuming infinite price elasticities of supply of imports and exports, the sum of the price elasticities of demand for imports and exports should exceed unity. In what follows we assume that the Marshall–Lerner conditions are always satisfied so that a depreciation of the domestic currency results in an increase in net exports and causes both the IS and BP curves to shift to the right. Finally, as before, net capital flows are held to be a function of the differential between the domestic and world interest rate.

We are now in a position to analyse the effect of a change in fiscal and monetary policy on income and the exchange rate within the Keynesian model.

2.4.1 The Effect of a Change in Fiscal and Monetary Policy on Income and the Exchange Rate

The effect of fiscal policy on real income and the exchange rate depends on the relative slopes of the BP and LM curves. This is illustrated for imperfect capital mobility in panels (a) and (b) of Figure 2.5, which are the floating counterparts of Figure 2.2 discussed earlier with respect to fixed exchange rates. Figures 2.5a illustrates the case where the BP curve is steeper than the LM curve, and 2.5b where the LM curve is steeper than the BP curve. In Figure 2.5a the economy is initially in equilibrium at point A, the triple intersection of IS_0 LM_0 and BP_0. Expansionary fiscal policy shifts the IS curve from IS_0 to IS_1. Under fixed exchange rates fiscal expansion would result in a balance of payments deficit (see section 2.2.2), i.e. IS_1 and LM_0 intersect at point B below BP_0. With flexible exchange rates the exchange rate adjusts to correct potential balance of payments disequilibria. An excess supply of domestic currency in the foreign exchange market causes the exchange rate to depreciate, shifting the IS_1 and BP_0 curves to the right until a new equilibrium is reached along the LM_0 curve to the right of B, for example at point C the triple intersection of IS_2 LM_0 and BP_1 with an income level of Y_1. In this particular case (BP curve steeper than the LM curve) the exchange rate depreciation reinforces the effects of domestic fiscal expansion on aggregate demand, leading to a higher level of output and employment. Turning to Figure 2.5b the initial equilibrium is again at point A, the triple intersection of IS_0 LM_0 and BP_0. Fiscal expansion shifts the IS curve outwards from IS_0 to IS_1 with the intersection of IS_1 and LM_0 at point B above BP_0. This is equivalent to a balance of payments surplus under fixed exchange rates and causes the exchange rate to adjust to eliminate the excess demand for domestic currency. In contrast to the analysis for Figure 2.5a, the exchange rate appreciates causing both the IS_1 and BP_0 curves to shift to the left. Equilibrium will be established along the LM curve to the left of point B, for example at point C. Thus fiscal policy will be less effective in influencing output and employment when the LM curve is steeper than the BP curve as fiscal expansion will

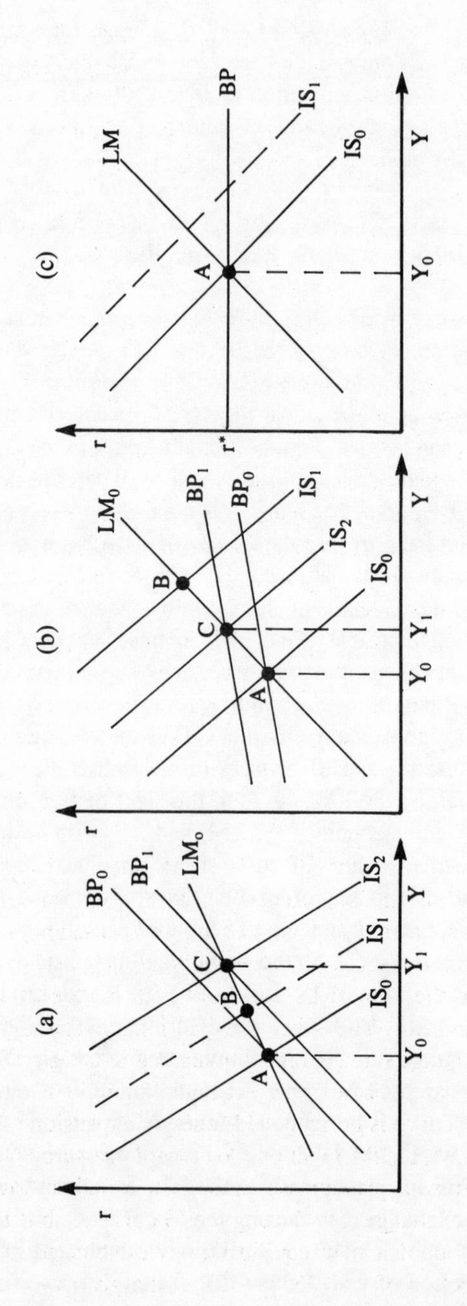

Figure 2.5 Fiscal expansion under (a) and (b) imperfect and (c) perfect capital mobility

cause the exchange rate to appreciate, partly offsetting the effects of fiscal expansion on aggregate demand. As noted earlier in the case of fixed exchange rates, Figure 2.5b is more likely to represent the true situation.

In the limiting case of perfect capital mobility illustrated in Figure 2.5c, fiscal policy becomes completely ineffective and is unable to affect output and employment. In the case of perfect capital mobility the BP curve is horizontal, i.e. the domestic rate of interest is tied to the rate ruling in the rest of the world at r^*. If the domestic rate of interest was to rise above the given world rate there would be an infinite capital inflow, and vice versa. Fiscal expansion (i.e. a shift in the IS curve to the right from IS_0 to IS_1) puts upwards pressure on the domestic interest rate. This incipient pressure results in an inflow of capital and leads to an appreciation of the exchange rate. As the exchange rate appreciates net exports decrease causing the IS curve to move back to the left. Equilibrium will be re-established at point A only when the capital inflows are large enough to appreciate the exchange rate sufficiently to shift the IS curve back to its original position. In other words fiscal expansion crowds out net exports and there is no change in output and employment. At the original income level Y_0 the current account deficit will have increased by exactly the same amount as the government budget deficit.

We now consider the effects of expansionary monetary policy on real income and the exchange rate. Figure 2.6a illustrates the effects of monetary expansion under imperfect capital mobility. The economy is initially in equilibrium at point A, the triple intersection of IS_0 LM_0 and BP_0. Monetary expansion shifts the LM curve from LM_0 to LM_1. Under fixed exchange rates this would result in a balance of payments deficit (see section 2.2.2), i.e. LM_1 and IS_0 intersect at point B below BP_0. With flexible exchange rates the exchange rate depreciates to maintain balance of payments equilibrium and both the BP and IS curves shift to the right until a new equilibrium is established along the curve LM_1 to the right of B, such as at point C, the triple intersection of IS_1 LM_1 and BP_1. The effect of expansionary monetary policy is reinforced by exchange rate depreciation leading to a higher level of real income. In the extreme case of perfect capital mobility illustrated in Figure 2.6b, the BP curve is horizontal. Monetary expansion (shift in the LM curve from LM_0 to LM_1) will put downward pressure on the domestic interest rate. This incipient pressure results in capital outflows and a depreciation of the exchange rate causing the IS curve to shift to the right (from IS_0 to IS_1) until a new equilibrium is established at point C, the triple intersection of LM_1 IS_1 and BP at the given world interest rate r^* and

Figure 2.6 Monetary expansion under (a) imperfect and (b) perfect capital mobility

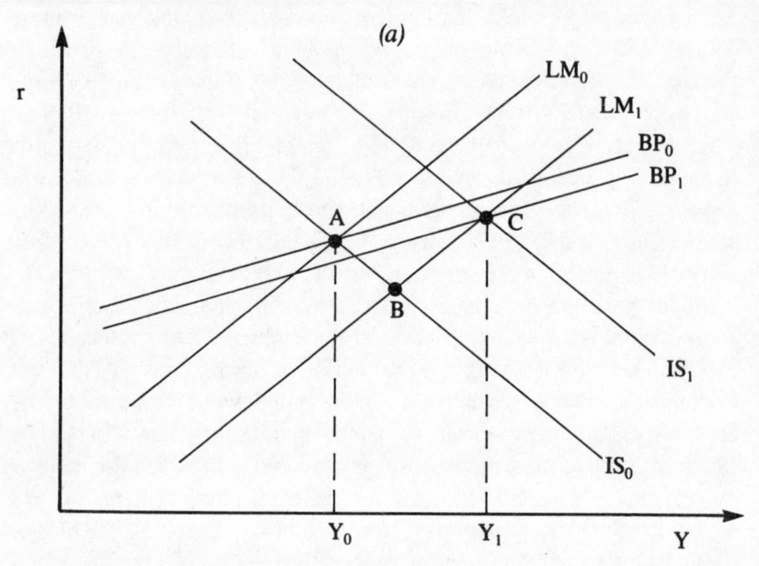

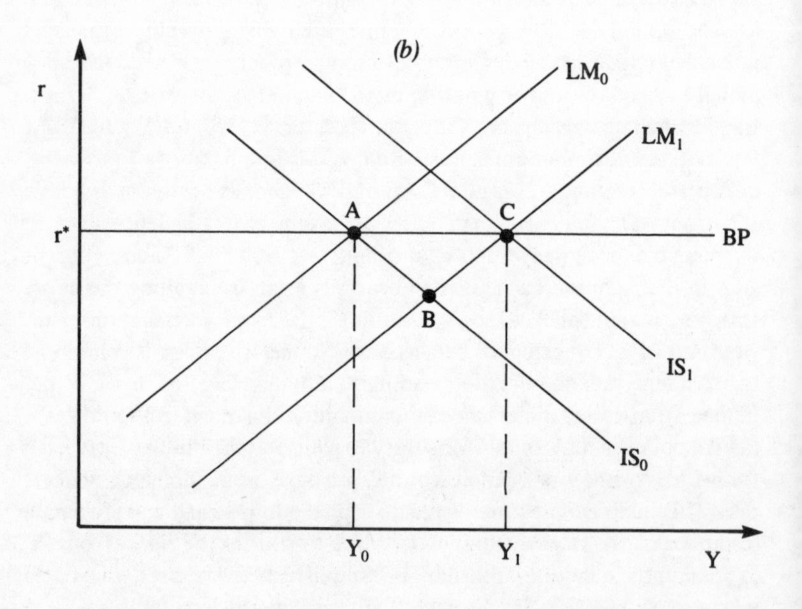

a new income level Y_1. In this case monetary policy is completely effective and contrasts with the position of fiscal policy discussed earlier.

In summary, the effects of fiscal policy on income and the exchange rate are ambiguous depending on the relative slopes of the LM and BP curves, whereas monetary expansion (contraction) results in an increase (decrease) in income and exchange rate depreciation (appreciation). Note equilibrium is always along the given LM curve because under floating exchange rates the domestic money supply is fixed by the authorities. Adjustment occurs because of changes in the exchange rate, which alters the position of the BP and IS curves.

2.4.2 Concluding Comments

In addition to the criticisms of this model noted in section 2.2.4, the reader should note two further problems with the above analysis. First, the effects of changes in the exchange rate on aggregate supply are neglected in the model. For example, as the exchange rate depreciates the home currency price of imports increases. This will affect the price of domestic goods if imports are used in their production and/or if workers press for higher nominal wage claims to protect their real wages. Secondly, expectations of exchange rate changes are neglected in the model. Capital movements, however, depend not only on the differential between domestic and foreign interest rates but also on expected exchange rate changes. As we will see, although the simple monetary approach also neglects expectations it is possible to incorporate a role for exchange rate expectations in determining the exchange rate in monetary models. We now turn to consider the monetary approach to exchange rate determination.

2.5 THE MONETARY APPROACH UNDER FLEXIBLE EXCHANGE RATES

The monetary approach to the determination of the exchange rate is a direct application of the monetary approach to the balance of payments to the case of flexible exchange rates (see Frenkel and Johnson 1978). You will recall from section 2.3 that in the fixed exchange rate case of the monetary approach the relationship between the stock demand for and supply of money is regarded as the main determinant of balance of payments flows. Further, that while the authorities control the volume of domestic credit the money supply is endogenous with balance of payments deficits/surpluses leading to predictable changes in the money supply through changes in international reserves. In the flexible exchange rate case of the monetary approach 'the proximate determinants of exchange rates...are the demand for and supply of various national monies' (Mussa 1976). Given the absence of balance of payments deficits/surpluses there are no reserve changes and the only source of monetary expansion is domestic credit expansion, which is determined by the authorities. Other things being equal, an increase in domestic credit under fixed exchange rates leads to a balance of payments deficit and an associated loss of international reserves, whereas under flexible exchange rates it leads to exchange rate depreciation and an increase in the domestic price level.

2.5.1 Monetary Models

A number of monetary models of exchange rates with different specifications have appeared in the literature. The key assumptions usually made in these models are the same as those noted in section 2.3.2, with the omission of the assumption concerning sterilization, since under a system of pure flexible exchange rates there is an absence of balance of payments surpluses/deficits.

The predictions of the monetary approach can be illustrated by way of a simple monetary model along the lines of that outlined in section 2.3.2. (At this stage it would be helpful to reread this section.) Suppose the authorities increase the domestic money supply, i.e. domestic credit. With real income fixed at its full employment or natural level, and the domestic interest rate tied to the world rate (by the law of one price) then the excess supply of money in the money market can only be eliminated by an increase in the domestic price level. In the case of a country that is too small to affect the world price level, the increase in the domestic price level results from a change in the exchange rate. Central to this analysis is the assumption of purchasing power parity (PPP) whereby the domestic and the world price level are the same when converted at the going exchange rate. In other words the two price levels are equal when expressed in the same currency. More formally, referring to equation (2.3),

$$P = e P^* \tag{2.3}$$

where i. P is the domestic price level
ii. P^* is the world price level, and
iii. e is the domestic currency price of one unit of foreign currency i.e. a rise in e is a depreciation of the domestic currency, and vice versa.

The excess supply of money results in an increased demand for foreign goods and securities and a corresponding excess supply of domestic currency on the foreign exchange market, causing the exchange rate to rise (remember that for our purposes the exchange rate is defined as the domestic currency price of one unit of foreign currency so that a rise in e is a depreciation of the domestic currency). In line with PPP (equation 2.3) the rise in e drives up the domestic price level and results in an increase in the demand for money, restoring money market equilibrium. For example, a 10 per cent increase in the money supply would lead to a 10 per cent depreciation of the domestic currency and a 10 per cent increase in the domestic price level; i.e. in line with equation (2.3), P rises in the same proportion as the rise in e.

The main feature of the simple monetary model outlined above is that the exchange rate is determined by the relative money supplies. In a two-country world where both countries increase their money supplies together by the same amount (e.g. 10 per cent) their price levels would also increase by the same amount (10 per cent) and there would be no change in the (real) exchange rate. In other words, the exchange rate is the relative price of the two moneys.

In slightly more complicated monetary models allowing for real income growth and also changes in foreign prices in response to world monetary changes, the monetary approach predicts that the rate of change of the exchange rate will depend on relative rates of monetary expansion and real income growth. Two interesting predictions derive from such models (for simplicity we assume a two-country world). First, *ceteris paribus*, if the rate of monetary expansion in the domestic country is greater than that overseas the exchange rate will depreciate (i.e. e will rise), and vice versa. Secondly, *ceteris paribus*, if real income growth is higher in the domestic country than overseas the exchange rate will appreciate (i.e. e will fall), and vice versa. In other words, a rapidly inflating country will experience a depreciating exchange rate, while a fast-growing country will experience an appreciating exchange rate. The reader should note that such predictions critically depend upon the assumptions of PPP, i.e. equation (2.3), holding.

The simple monetary approach to the analysis of exchange rate determination outlined above has been subjected to a number of cricitisms directed, in part, to the assumptions underlying monetary models. One criticism which can be taken on board is the neglect in the simple approach of exchange rate expectations in determining the exchange rate. In what follows we consider how the predictions from monetary models which incorporate exchange rate expectations differ from those of the simple monetary model.

Our starting point is the international asset market. The relative return on domestic and foreign assets has two components – the coupon interest yield and any expected capital gain/loss due to expected exchange rate changes. In equilibrium the expected return on domestic and foreign assets must be equal or else funds would be moved and the exchange rate would change. A detailed discussion of the nature of interest parity is beyond our present scope and in what follows we adopt the form referred to as uncovered interest parity (UIP) as being a characteristic assumption of monetary models UIP implies:

$$r - r^{*} = x \tag{2.4}$$

where i. r is the domestic interest rate
ii. r^{*} is the foreign interest rate, and
iii. x is the expected rate of depreciation of the domestic currency.

In other words, expected exchange rate changes have to be compensated by the interest rate differential between domestic and foreign assets.

We now briefly examine the significance of incorporating exchange rate expectations (assuming the rational expectations hypothesis which is discussed in the appendix to Chapter 3) into the monetary model (via UIP) as far as domestic monetary policy is concerned. Suppose the authorities increase the domestic money supply. In the simple monetary model analysed above the exchange rate increases (depreciates) in proportion to the increase in the money supply. This equiproportionate relationship will, however, be disturbed if the increase in the money supply affects economic agents' expectations about future monetary policy and therefore exchange rate expectations. A change in exchange rate expectations will affect the domestic interest rate (via UIP), which in turn affects the demand for money and therefore the exchange rate (via PPP). For example, if exchange rate expectations are revised upwards (i.e. an expected depreciation) the rise in the domestic interest rate (via UIP) will tend to reduce the demand for money thereby reinforcing the rise in the exchange rate (via PPP) resulting from the increase in the money supply. In other words in this particular example the exchange rate will rise (depreciate) by proportionately more than the increase in the money supply in the current time period.

2.5.2 Concluding Comments

In contrast to the fixed-price/less than full employment Keynesian model the monetary model assumes domestic prices are perfectly flexible with real income at its full employment or natural level. In the next section we consider exchange rate models which provide somewhat different insights into the analysis of exchange rate adjustment and allow for the possibility of exchange rate overshooting before equilibrium is reached in the long run. We begin by examining the implications of a model put forward by Dornbusch (1976), which is Keynesian in the sense that the domestic price level is sticky in the short run, but neoclassical in the sense that real income tends towards its natural level in the long run, a level determined independently of monetary policy. In contrast to commodity prices which are 'sticky', the prices of financial assets are assumed to adjust immediately to changed circumstances.

2.6 EXCHANGE RATE MODELS AND OVERSHOOTING

2.6.1 The Dornbusch Model

The Dornbusch model is in essence a monetary model with rational expectations and imperfect price flexibility. Critical to the discussion which follows are the assumptions that: (i) goods prices are sticky (i.e. goods markets adjust slowly) so that PPP is violated in the short run and (ii) uncovered interest parity (UIP) always holds. As we will see, the implications of these assumptions in terms of macroeconomic policy and the short-run behaviour of the exchange rate is that expansionary monetary policy results in the exchange rate temporarily overshooting its long-run equilibrium level and that while monetary policy is neutral in the long run, in the short run it has real effects.

Consider what happens following an increase in the domestic money supply if goods prices are sticky in the short run but interest rates and exchange rates adjust instantaneously to a monetary disturbance. In the short run with fixed prices and a given natural level of output an increase in the (real) money supply results in a fall in the domestic interest rate, thereby maintaining equilibrium in the money market. The fall in the domestic interest rate (r) means that with the foreign interest rate (r^*) fixed exogenously (due to the small-country assumption) the domestic currency must be expected to appreciate for UIP to hold, i.e. x must be negative in equation (2.4). In this way equilibrium in the international bond market is maintained. While short-run equilibrium requires an expected appreciation of the domestic currency, long-run equilibrium requires an actual depreciation of the home currency in line with PPP, i.e. e must rise in equation (2.3). This apparent inconsistency can be reconciled if the exchange rate immediately depreciates to a point from which it can be expected to appreciate. In other words, since long-run equilibrium requires a depreciation of the domestic currency (compared to its initial level) the exchange rate depreciates too far (i.e. in the short run it overshoots) so that it can be expected to appreciate back to its long-run equilibrium level. In the converse case, following a contraction in the domestic money supply the exchange rate would over-appreciate. Such short-run overshooting is fully consistent with rational expectations because the exchange rate follows the path it is expected to follow.

A number of points are worth noting about the above analysis. First, the source of overshooting in the Dornbusch model lies in goods prices being relatively sticky in the short run. In other words, the crucial assumption made in the model is that asset markets adjust more quickly than do goods markets, i.e. goods prices are sticky in the short run. Secondly, the rate at which the exchange rate adjusts back to its long-run equilibrium level depends on the speed at which the price level adjusts. Finally, an increase in the money supply is likely to cause output to rise (temporarily) above its natural level in the short run because as the exchange rate depreciates too far domestic goods become relatively cheap, increasing competitiveness and stimulating aggregate demand. Once prices have fully adjusted output will return to its natural level so that monetary policy is again neutral in the long run.

2.6.2 Portfolio Models

Before concluding this chapter, mention should be made of some recent developments in exchange rate literature. In the past decade and a half a considerable number of models (e.g. Branson and Buiter 1983) have been developed which take account of portfolio or asset-market equilibrium in the analysis of exchange rates. The discussion which follows is designed to outline essential distinguishing characteristics of these models and the insight they provide into the dynamics of exchange rate adjustment. The interested reader is referred to the more detailed exposition contained in, for example, Copeland (1989).

Portfolio balance models are similar to the Dornbusch model discussed in section 2.6.1. However two differences are significant. First, the assumption is made that agents are risk averse, with the consequence that risk premiums exist so that UIP (equation 2.4) does not hold. Secondly, a richer menu of assets is available for wealth holders. The portfolio balance model is therefore more general than either the Dornbusch or monetary models, which can be regarded as special cases of this more general model. The conclusion derived from these two differences is that wealth holders will diversify asset holdings in a similar manner to that discussed in Chapter 4 section 4.4.3 for money holdings based on Tobin's risk aversion analysis.

A typical simple portfolio can be assumed to consist of domestic money (M) domestic bonds (B) and net overseas assets (eF) where F is the value denoted in foreign currency and e is the exchange rate – units of domestic currency per unit of foreign currency. Portfolio equilibrium can be derived by solving the following system of asset-demand equations together with the specification for financial wealth (W).

$$M/W = m(r_M; r_B; r^* + x) \quad m_1 > 0; m_2, m_3 < 0 \tag{2.5}$$

$$B/W = b(r_M; r_B; r^* + x) \quad b_1, b_3 < 0; b_2 > 0 \tag{2.6}$$

$$eF = f(r_M; r_B; r^* + x) \quad f_1, f_2 < 0; f_3 > 0 \tag{2.7}$$

$$W = M + B + eF \tag{2.8}$$

where r_M, r_B are the returns on domestic money and bonds respectively and $r^* + x$ (as defined in equation 2.4) the return on foreign assets. The signs on the coefficients represent the view that asset demand will react positively to an increase in the own interest rate but negatively to increases in cross interest rates.

Changes in financial wealth (W) arise from two sources. Increases in the quantity of wealth arise from (i) the public sector deficit and

(ii) the acquisition of foreign assets, i.e. the capital account which is the mirror image of the current account surplus. A second change in financial wealth arises from valuation effects. In respect of domestic assets a rise in r_B reduces the market value of B. Similarly a rise in e (appreciation of the foreign currency) raises the market value of overseas assets. In a static model without growth long-run equilibrium therefore requires both the public sector deficit and the current account of the balance of payments to be zero so that both the total and composition of wealth is constant. The reader will note the wide variety of channels through which shocks affect the exchange rate, i.e. through changes in (i) asset demands, (ii) wealth, and (iii) the impact of valuation changes in wealth. Also, unlike the models discussed earlier, it is significant that the current account balance itself, as opposed to the overall balance of payments, plays an important role in exchange rate determination.

As will be noted in Chapter 4 section 4.5, portfolio balance models are difficult to handle analytically and are consequently beyond the scope of this text. We shall therefore restrict our analysis to an intuitive illustration of the impact of an increase in the money supply brought about by purchase of domestic bonds (i.e. an open market operation). We start from a situation of full equilibrium where all asset markets clear and the current account is in balance with a zero balance of trade. In the short run an increase in the money supply causes the exchange rate to depreciate, resulting in a current account surplus. A current account surplus must be matched by a capital account deficit (so that the two accounts sum to zero) and involves domestic residents accumulating foreign assets. The resultant increase in domestic wealth in turn affects (positively) both asset demands for money, bonds and foreign assets and also domestic expenditure. In the short run the effect has been to reduce the domestic rate of interest and cause the foreign currency to appreciate (i.e. the domestic currency to depreciate). As we have seen, long-run equilibrium requires a zero current balance so that it may be assumed that long-run equilibrium would be the same as that discussed for the monetary approach in section 2.5, where the domestic currency depreciates in the same proportion as the increase in the money supply. Yet this is not the case, as we shall now see.

The increase in the money supply of say 10 per cent, for example, causes the price level to rise by 10 per cent. However, the domestic currency depreciates by less than 10 per cent so that the real exchange rate (e/P) appreciates. To understand why this is so it is merely necessary to recognize that the current account surplus noted in the short-run adjustment will have produced positive investment in overseas assets and therefore positive and recurring increases in investment income. This means that a zero current account balance will require a negative trade balance (imports greater than exports) to offset the positive investment income. Hence the exchange rate will not depreciate to the full extent (10 per cent) to restore a zero balance of trade. In summary, the competitiveness of the economy has been eroded by an appreciation of the real exchange rate and this produces the balance of trade deficit. Because of the continued assumption of slow adjustment in the goods market and fast adjustment in the financial markets, the nominal exchange rate (e) will overshoot its equilibrium value, as in the Dornbusch model.

2.7 CONCLUSION

In this chapter we have considered the role the external environment plays in influencing macroeconomic policy in an open economy. Our discussion has focused on the different insights provided by the various approaches within the context of the two polar cases of fixed and pure floating exchange rates. In fact since the early 1970s the policy environment provided by managed or dirty exchange rates has meant that macroeconomic policy has had a bearing on both the balance of payments and the exchange rate. In the next chapter we turn to consider the central policy issues of macroeconomics, namely inflation and unemployment.

3. Inflation and Unemployment

3.1 INTRODUCTION

The main purpose of this chapter is twofold: (i) to consider the controversy over the relationship between inflation and unemployment commonly referred to as the Phillips curve, and (ii) to consider the policy implications of the Phillips curve analysis. To this end we begin with a discussion of the original Phillips curve (section 3.2) before discussing how the basic Phillips curve has been subsequently augmented (section 3.3) and finally ending with a review of the policy implications of the expectations-augmented Phillips curve (section 3.4).

3.2 THE PHILLIPS CURVE

The inverse (non-linear) relationship between the level of unemployment and wage inflation, popularly known as the Phillips curve, is one of the most famous relationships in macroeconomics. The original study undertaken by Phillips (1958) investigated the statistical relationship between unemployment and the rate of change of money wage rates in the UK over the period 1861–1957. For the period 1861–1913 Phillips was able to estimate an inverse relationship between unemployment (U) and the rate of change of money wages ($\dot{W}$) which could predict accurately the relationship between the two variables for the period 1951–7. The estimated average relationship was non-linear and appeared to show that at an unemployment level of approximately 5.5 per cent the rate of change of money wages was zero. Furthermore at an unemployment level of approximately 2.5 per cent the rate of change of money wages was approximately equal to the then-average growth of productivity of 2 per cent (see Figure 3.1). In consequence an unemployment level of 2.5 per cent was compatible with stable prices.

The Phillips curve was quickly adopted by economists because it provided both rare evidence of a stable relationship between two variables

Figure 3.1 The Phillips curve

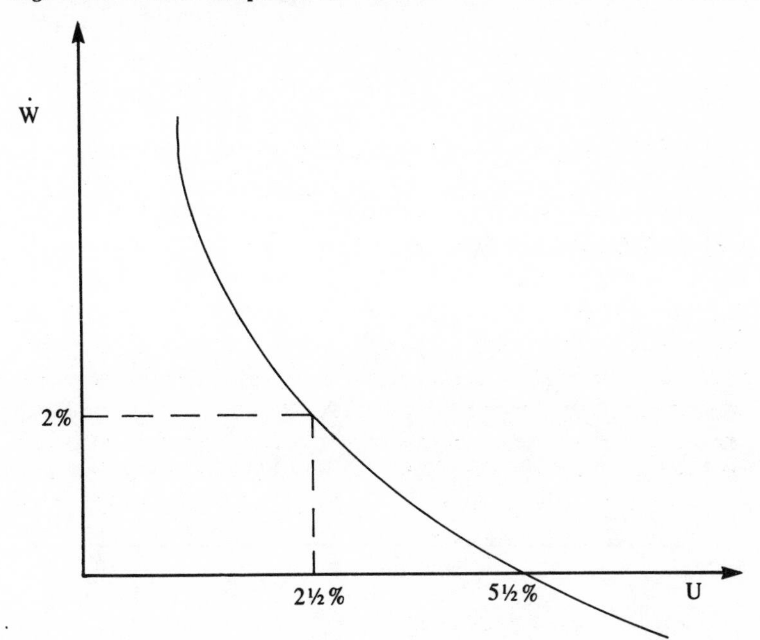

that had existed for almost a century and an insight into the problem facing policy-makers of simultaneously achieving high levels of employment with price stability given the trade-off between wage inflation and unemployment.

Phillips's study was a statistical investigation, and the economic rationale for the curve was provided subsequently by Lipsey (1960). Lipsey argued that within a single market the speed at which wages rise (or fall) depends linearly on the degree of excess demand for (or supply of) labour in that market. This is illustrated in Figure 3.2. Panel (a) uses standard demand and supply analysis and shows that at any money wage rate below W_e there is excess demand for labour. For example, at wage rate W_1 there is excess demand for labour of aa (equal to Oa in panel b) while at W_2 there is excess demand for labour of bb (equal to Ob in panel b). Lipsey argued that wages would rise in conditions of excess demand and furthermore that the rate of increase in money wage rates would be faster the larger the excess demand for labour. This

Figure 3.2 The relationship between wage change and excess demand

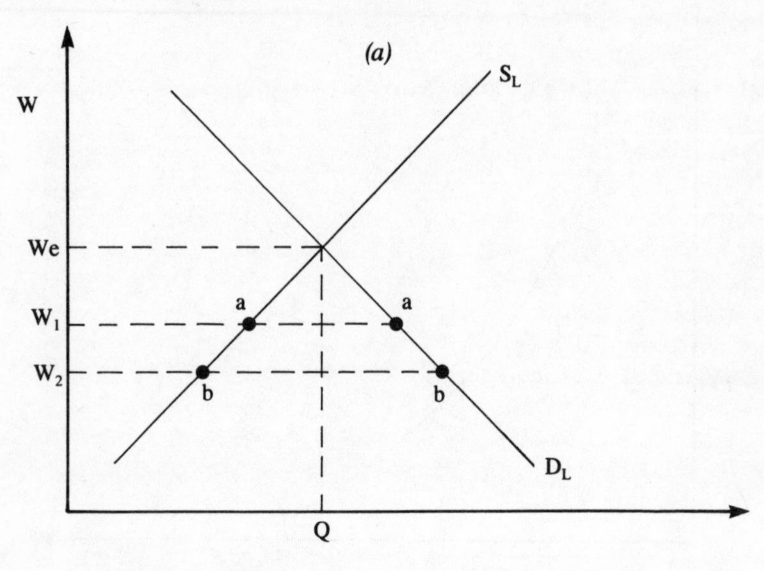

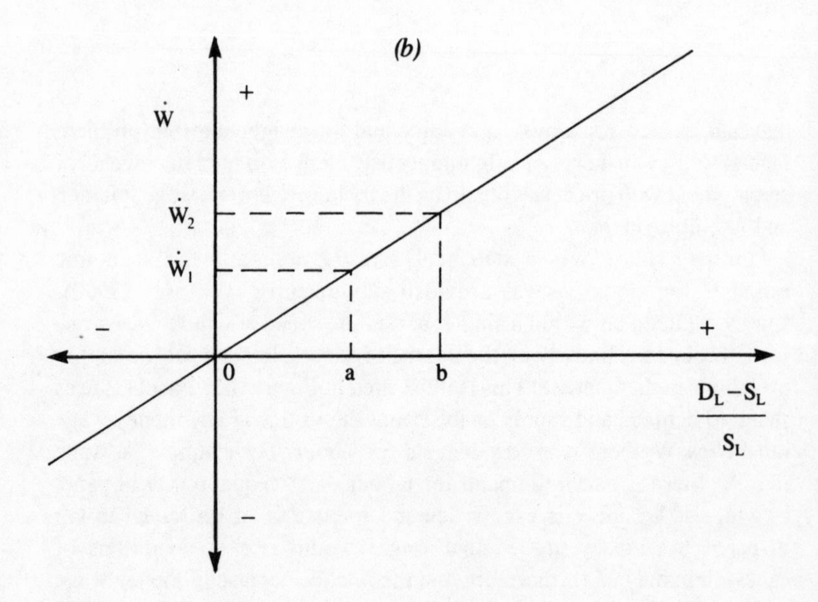

latter relationship is depicted in linear form in panel (b) of Figure 3.2 where the excess demand for labour is specified in percentage form. The problem for quantification of this reaction function is that since excess demand for labour is not directly observable it was necessary to use a proxy or surrogate measure for excess demand. In this connection Lipsey postulated an inverse non-linear relationship between excess demand and unemployment. Figure 3.3 illustrates how an excess supply of labour will manifest itself in unemployment. Even when the demand for and supply of labour are equal (i.e. zero excess demand – point a in Figure 3.3) some positive amount of frictional unemployment exists as individuals change jobs and search for new employment. Lipsey argued that although unemployment would fall in response to positive excess demand as jobs become easier to find (e.g. as vacancies increase) registered unemployment would only asymptotically approach zero. In other words Lipsey postulated that a steadily increasing excess demand

Figure 3.3 The relationship between excess demand for labour and unemployment

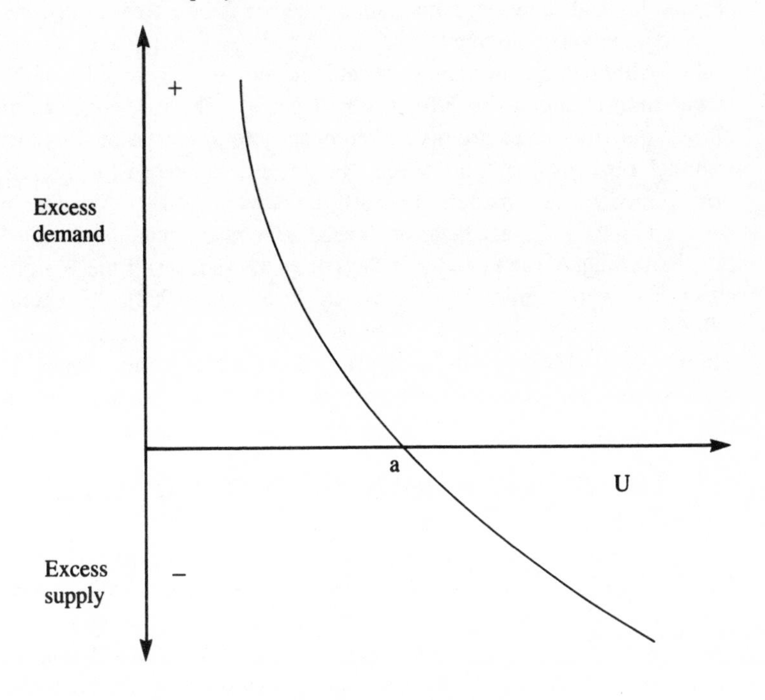

would be accompanied by increasingly smaller reductions in unemployment.

Lipsey provided the theoretical justification for the Phillips curve through the combination of two postulated relationships: that of (i) a positive linear relationship between the rate of increase in money wages and excess demand, and (ii) an inverse non-linear relationship between excess demand and unemployment. Combining these relationships provided the rationale for the non-linear inverse relationship between the rate of increase of money wages and unemployment in a single market with a positive amount of frictional or search unemployment required for zero growth in money wages. Aggregation over all markets produced the macro Phillips curve.

By the late 1960s the basic Phillips curve relationship appeared to have broken down, with many countries experiencing the simultaneous occurrence of rising unemployment and rising rates of inflation. Not only was the Phillips curve inconsistent with the facts but at the theoretical level the analysis underlying the curve was also heavily criticized. Orthodox microeconomic theory of the labour market suggested that the demand for and supply of labour should be specified in real terms, but the foregoing version of the Phillips curve referred to nominal or money wages. Although money wages are set in negotiations, both sides of the labour market attempt to influence real wages. The two concepts of money and real wages are only interchangeable in conditions of price stability. Furthermore, since wage bargains are negotiated for discrete time periods what matters to both employers and employees in determining the real wage being negotiated is the rate of inflation expected to exist throughout the period of the contract. As a result the Phillips curve has been augmented, notably by Friedman (1968) and Phelps (1968), by the introduction of the expected rate of inflation as an additional variable determining the rate of change of money wages. In what follows we focus on the arguments put forward by Friedman.

3.3 THE EXPECTATIONS-AUGMENTED PHILLIPS CURVE

Introducing the expected rate of inflation whilst still maintaining the axes of the rate of increase in money wages ($\dot{W}$) and unemployment (U) results in not one unique macro Phillips curve but instead a whole family of such curves, each curve being associated with a different expected rate of inflation. Each level of unemployment corresponds to a unique rate of change of real wages. As the expected rate of inflation increases so the Phillips curve shifts upwards. This is illustrated diagrammatically in Figure 3.4. For simplicity, in what follows we will make the assumption that the growth of productivity remains constant at zero so that any change in money wages is ultimately matched by a corresponding change in prices.

Figure 3.4 *The expectations-augmented Phillips curve*

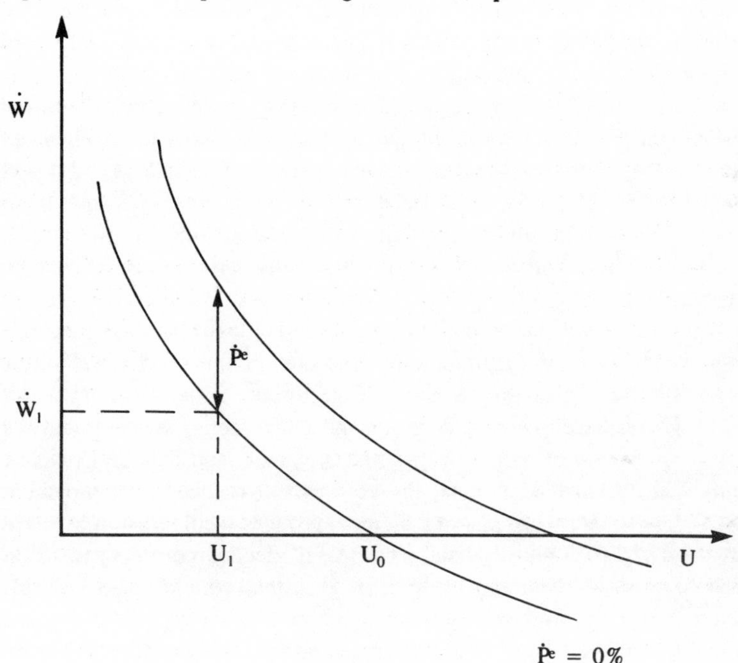

Equilibrium initially occurs at U_0 with a zero rate of wage increase so that with the assumption of zero growth in productivity the price level would be constant and the expected rate of inflation ($\dot{P}^e$) would also be zero. If the government expanded aggregate demand so that unemployment fell to U_1 then the rate of wage increase would rise to $\dot{W}_1$ and prices would increase by the rate of increase of money wages (i.e. $\dot{P} = \dot{W}_1$). The assumption made by Friedman is that expectations adjust slowly to changed circumstances, particularly after a period of price stability. In the following analysis we will assume that slow adjustment of expectations can be adequately represented by the adaptive expectations model (see the appendix to this chapter) by which expectations of future rates of inflation are revised by a proportion of the difference between the actual rate of inflation ($\dot{P}$) and the expected rate of inflation ($\dot{P}^e$). If price expectations are formed according to the adaptive expectations hypothesis then sooner or later workers would start to expect future price increases and would take their expectations into consideration when entering into wage negotiations. This means that if a real wage increase of $\dot{W}_1$ is required money wages would have to rise at a rate of $\dot{W}_1$ plus the expected rate of inflation. In other words the short-run Phillips curve would shift upwards. The crucial question is how far it shifts. If the actual rate of inflation is completely anticipated in wage bargains then the gap between the two curves in Figure 3.4 will equal $\dot{W}_1 = \dot{P}^e$. As we will next discuss, this means that if there is no money illusion the short-run Phillips curve will shift upwards with $\dot{P} = \dot{P}^e$ and there will be no long-run trade-off between unemployment and inflation.

Complete anticipation of actual inflation is illustrated in Figure 3.5, where for ease of diagrammatic presentation the short-run Phillips curves are assumed to be linear. Equilibrium initially occurs at U_0 (i.e. where there is zero excess demand in the labour market) with the rate of increase of money wages and the actual and expected rates of inflation all equal at zero. If the government reduced unemployment to U_1 by monetary expansion then money wages would start to increase at a rate of 2 per cent per annum. The initial effect of monetary expansion would be to increase aggregate demand in the economy, and as firms increased their production to meet this increase in aggregate demand the demand for labour would increase and unemployment fall. Money wages would start to increase at a rate of 2 per cent due to the increased demand for labour. The supply of labour would also respond to the increased demand because, having recently experienced a period of price stability (i.e. $\dot{P} = \dot{P}^e = 0$ per cent), workers would interpret the increase in their money wages as an increase in their real wages. Maintaining the assumption of no growth in productivity, a 2 per cent rate of wage inflation wouid lead to a 2 per cent rate of price inflation. If the rate of price inflation is fully anticipated by employers and employees money wages would then have to increase by 4 per cent to maintain the 2 per cent rise in real wages required by the continued

Figure 3.5 Short-run Phillips curves and the vertical long-run Phillips curve

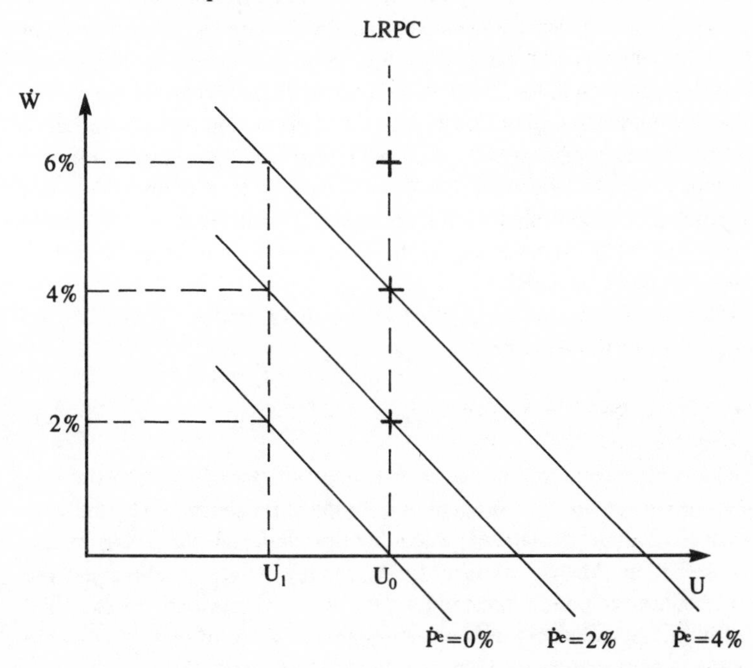

existence of excess demand in the labour market. This would require a further increase in the rate of monetary expansion to finance a 4 per cent rate of wage and therefore price inflation. The short-run Phillips curve would shift upwards as individuals revised upwards their expectations of future rates of inflation. In the following period money wages would then have to rise by 6 per cent to attain the necessary 2 per cent increase in real wages and so on, necessitating further increases in the rate of monetary expansion. In contrast, if the authorities refused to increase further the rate of monetary expansion the rising price level would reduce the real value of the money supply. Unemployment would rise until such time as, in equilibrium, the rate of expansion of the money supply exactly equalled the percentage increase in the actual and expected rates of inflation and unemployment would return to U_0. If all such points of equilibrium are joined together we obtain the long-run Phillips curve, which is vertical in the case where actual inflation is completely anticipated. At U_0 the rate of increase in money wages is exactly equalled by the rate of increase in prices so that the real wage is constant, with the result that there would be no disturbance in the labour market. Similarly, the real value of the money supply would also remain constant so that there would be no disturbance in the money market. U_0 has been termed the natural rate of unemployment by Friedman (1968) and is the only level of unemployment at which a constant rate of inflation may be maintained. An alternative term used for the natural rate is the 'non-accelerating inflation rate of unemployment' (NAIRU).

Mathematically the expectations-augmented Phillips curve can be expressed by the equation:

$$\dot{W} = f(U) + \beta \dot{P}^e \tag{3.1}$$

The monetarist view is that in the long run $\beta = 1$, so that the rate of money wage increase is equal to a component determined by the state of excess demand plus the expected rate of inflation. If there is no excess demand then the rate of increase of money wages would equal the expected rate of inflation and only in the special case where the expected rate of inflation is zero would wage inflation be zero. In summary, within the monetarist school: (i) inflation is held to be caused by excess demand, due primarily to excessive monetary expansion, and expectations regarding future rates of inflation and (ii) there is no long-run trade-off between unemployment and inflation (i.e. the long-run Phillips curve is vertical) but only a short-term benefit achieved at the expense of a permanently higher rate of inflation.

We now consider what happens if economic agents do not fully anticipate the rate of inflation in their negotiations. In this situation the short-run Phillips curves in Figure 3.5 would not shift up by the full amount of the actual rate of inflation. The coefficient β in equation (3.1) would be less than 1 with the result that the slope of the long-run Phillips curve would be steeper than that of the short-run curve but less than vertical. In this case there would be a permanent trade-off between inflation and unemployment but a less favourable one than that predicted by movement along the short-run Phillips curve. This is illustrated in Figure 3.6. Many Keynesians believe that the long-run Phillips curve is not vertical so that it is possible to pursue an unemployment target below U_0 but at the cost of a higher rate of wage inflation than that

Figure 3.6 The long-run Phillips curve

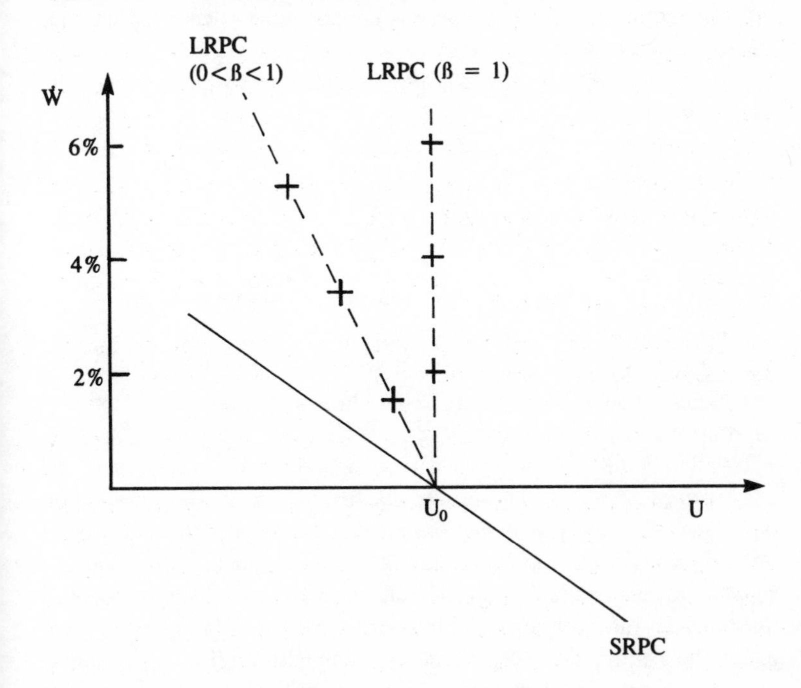

predicted by the short-run Phillips curve. It is also interesting to note that given that some Keynesians assign a role to wage increases made independently of the state of excess demand they have argued that the trade-off could be improved by some kind of direct controls operating on wages. In other words many Keynesians believe that the long-run (non-vertical) Phillips curve could be shifted downwards by the adoption of a prices and incomes policy, thereby achieving a lower rate of inflation at any given target level of unemployment.

Before we turn to discuss the policy implications of the expectations-augmented Phillips curve in more detail, it is worth noting that the empirical evidence from studies that have sought to test whether the coefficient for β is significantly different from unity is far from clear cut and the issue of the possible existence of a long-run vertical Phillips curve remains controversial. In summary, it would appear that there is sufficient evidence to sustain monetarists in their belief that β equals unity so that there would be no trade-off between unemployment and inflation in the long run, but there is not enough evidence to convince all the sceptics.

We now turn to discuss the policy implications of the expectations-augmented Phillips curve.

3.4 POLICY IMPLICATIONS

3.4.1 The Scope for Short-run Output-employment Gains

The belief in a vertical long-run Phillips curve implies that an increase in the rate of monetary growth can reduce unemployment below the natural rate only because the resulting inflation is unexpected. As soon as inflation is fully anticipated it will be incorporated into wage bargains and unemployment will return to the natural rate. The assumption underlying this analysis is that expected inflation adjusts to the actual inflation rate only gradually. In fact it is the existence of this time gap between an increase in the actual rate of inflation and the increase in the expected rate that permits a temporary reduction in unemployment below the natural rate. The economy eventually returns to its natural rate of unemployment but with a higher equilibrium wage and price inflation equal to the rate of monetary growth. Friedman envisages a lag of approximately 24 months before full adjustment takes place. Initially after a lag of some 6–9 months output increases and some 6–9 months later prices start to rise because of the increase in output. This causes output to return towards its previous (i.e. natural) level so that after a period of 24 months or so the main effect of an increase in the rate of monetary growth is on the prices, not output.

If, however, expectations are formed according to the rational expectations hypothesis (discussed more fully in the appendix to this chapter), and economic agents have access to the same information as the authorities, the expected rate of inflation will rise immediately in response to an increased rate of monetary expansion. In this case the authorities would be powerless to influence output and employment even in the short run because there would be no lag between an increase in the actual and expected rate of inflation, i.e. money is neutral in the short run. This is the view of the new classical school outlined in Chapter 1, section 1.3.3.

3.4.2 The Natural Rate of Unemployment and Supply-side Policies

A second important policy implication of the belief in a vertical long-run Phillips curve concerns employment policy. Within neoclassical analysis the natural rate of unemployment is associated with equilibrium in the labour market and hence with the structure of real wage rates. Friedman (1968), for example, has argued that the natural rate is dependent upon:

> the actual structural characteristics of the labor and commodity markets, including market imperfections, stochastic variability in demands and supplies, the cost of gathering information about job vacancies and labor availabilities, the costs of mobility, and so on.

According to this approach if governments wish to reduce the natural rate of unemployment in order to achieve higher employment levels they should pursue microeconomic, or what are referred to as supply-side, policies designed to improve the structure of the labour market and industry rather than macroeconomic policies. Although a discussion of potential microeconomic policies is outside the scope of our book it is interesting to note that over recent years a wide range of (often very controversial) policy measures have been advocated including measures designed to increase: (i) the flexibility of wages and working practices (e.g. by reducing trade union power); (ii) the incentive to work (e.g. through tax and social security reforms); (iii) the geographical mobility of labour (e.g. greater financial assistance to help cover the costs of moving) and the occupational mobility of labour (e.g. greater provision of government retraining schemes); and (iv) the efficiency of markets for capital (e.g. through the abolition of various controls on activity in financial markets) and goods and services (e.g. by privatization).

3.4.3 Accelerating Monetary Growth and Inflation

The monetarist belief in a vertical long-run Phillips curve further implies that any attempt to maintain unemployment below the natural rate will require the authorities to increase continuously the rate of monetary expansion and therefore accept a continuously rising rate of inflation. In order to maintain unemployment below the natural rate real wages must be kept below their equilibrium level. For this to happen prices would have to rise at a faster rate than money wages, but in this case employees would revise upwards their expectations of inflation and press for higher wage increases so that the end result would be an accelerating rate of wage increase (in terms of Figure 3.5, from 2 per cent to 4 per cent etc.) In summary, any attempt to maintain unemployment permanently below the natural rate will require accelerating monetary growth and will result in an accelerating rate of inflation. Conversely, if unemployment is pushed permanently above the natural rate accelerating deflation will occur.

We now turn to discuss the final policy implication of the expectations-augmented Phillips curve, namely the output/employment costs of reducing inflation. We begin with a discussion of the orthodox monetarist approach to this controversial question.

3.4.4 Output/Employment Costs of Reducing Inflation

Monetarists argue that inflation can only be reduced by slowing down the rate of monetary expansion. Reducing the rate of monetary expansion

Figure 3.7 The costs of reducing inflation: alternative policy options

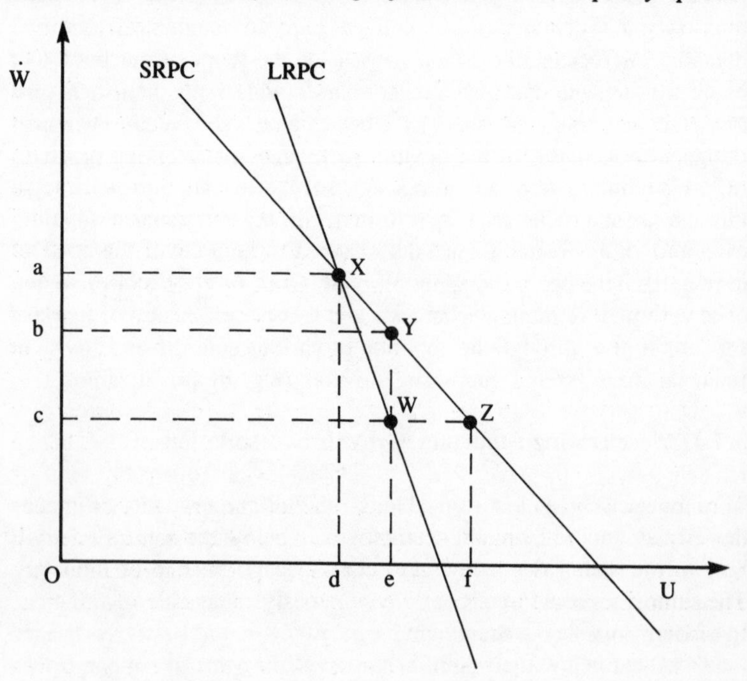

results in an increase in the level of unemployment. The more rapidly the authorities seek to reduce inflation the higher will be the costs in terms of unemployment. This particular policy dilemma facing the authorities is illustrated in Figure 3.7. In order to emphasize that this result in no way depends on the existence of a vertical long-run Phillips curve, Figure 3.7 depicts a long-run Phillips curve (LRPC) which, although steeper than the short-run Phillips curve (SRPC), is still not vertical.

Assume the economy is initially operating at point X, the intersection of SRPC and LRPC, i.e. the initial starting position is both a short- and long-run equilibrium situation where wage inflation equals Oa and unemployment Od. Now suppose the rate of wage inflation is too high for the authorities' liking and that they wish to reduce the rate of increase of money wages (and hence the rate of inflation) and move to position W on the LRPC where wage inflation equals Oc and unemployment equals Oe. Consider the two extreme policy options open to the authorities to move to their preferred position at W. One option would be to reduce dramatically the rate of monetary expansion and raise unemployment to Of so that wage inflation fell to Oc, i.e. an initial movement along SRPC from point X to Z. The initial cost of this option would be a relatively large increase in unemployment from Od to Of. As the actual rate of inflation fell below the expected rate and expectations of future rates of inflation were revised in a downwards direction, the short-run Phillips curve would shift downwards so that unemployment would eventually fall to Oe and a new short- and long-run equilibrium would eventually be achieved at point W. The other extreme policy option open to the authorities would be to gradually reduce the rate of monetary expansion and initially increase unemployment to Oe so that wage inflation fell to Ob, i.e. an initial movement along SRPC from point X to Y. This particular option would involve a much smaller initial increase in unemployment from Od to Oe. As before, as the actual rate of inflation fell below the expected rate (but to a much lesser extent) and expectations were revised downwards, the short-run Phillips curve would again move downwards but the transition to point W on the LRPC would take a much longer time span than under the first policy option considered above. The authorities could of course follow some compromise between these two polar policy options.

Nevertheless, the dilemma the authorities face is that the more rapidly they seek to reduce inflation the higher will be the cost in terms of unemployment. Recognition of this fact has led some orthodox monetarists to advocate a gradual reduction in the rate of monetary expansion in order to minimize the output/employment cost of reducing inflation. This type of policy entails living with inflation for quite long periods of time and has led some monetarists to advocate supplementary policy measures to accompany the gradual adjustment process to a lower rate of inflation.

Some monetarists (e.g. Friedman 1974) have advocated indexation as a method for reducing inflationary expectations and reducing the extent and duration of unemployment that accompanies a reduction in the rate of monetary expansion. For example, with indexation money wage rate increases would automatically fall as the rate of inflation fell. This would remove the danger that employers would be committed under existing contracts to excessive money wage increases when the rate of inflation declined. Wage rate increases would be less rapid and unemployment would rise by a smaller amount. In a similar manner some monetarists believe that a prices and incomes policy may have a role to play as a temporary and supplementary policy measure to monetary contraction designed to assist the transition to a lower rate of inflation by reducing inflationary expectations. In terms of the expectations-augmented Phillips curve analysis, if a prices and incomes policy succeeded in reducing inflationary expectations the short-run Phillips curve would shift downwards, enabling adjustment to a lower rate of inflation to be achieved both more quickly and at the cost of a lower level of unemployment. However, one of the problems with prices and incomes policy is that once the policy begins to break down or is ended inflationary expectations may be revised upwards, shifting the short-run Phillips curve upwards thereby offsetting the initial benefit of the policy in terms of lower unemployment and wage inflation. For example, a study of incomes policy and wage inflation for the UK between 1961 and 1977 by Henry and Ormerod (1978) concluded that:

> Whilst some incomes policies have reduced the rate of wage inflation during the period in which they operated, this reduction has only been temporary. Wage increases in the period immediately following the ending of policies were higher than they would otherwise have been, and these increases match losses incurred during the operation of the incomes policy.

In summary, within the orthodox monetarist approach the extent and duration of the rise in unemployment/loss of output following monetary contraction depends upon: (i) whether the authorities pursue a gradual or rapid reduction in the rate of monetary expansion; (ii) the extent of institutional adaptions (e.g. whether wage contracts are indexed) and

(iii) how quickly people adjust their expectations of future rates of inflation.

In contrast to orthodox monetarism the new classical approach suggests that the output/employment costs of reducing inflation will be negligible provided the policy of reducing the rate of monetary expansion is credible. New classical macroeconomics incorporates the monetarist belief that inflation is essentially a monetary phenomenon propagated by excessive monetary growth and can only be reduced by slowing down the rate of growth of the money supply. However, unlike orthodox monetarism the new classical approach suggests that an announced/anticipated reduction in the rate of monetary expansion will have little or no effect on the level of output and employment even in the short run. An announced and believed reduction in the rate of monetary growth would cause rational economic agents to revise quickly their inflation expectations in a downward direction according to the anticipated effects of the monetary contraction so that any fall in output and employment would be small and temporary, i.e. the downward shift of the short-run Phillips curve would be almost immediate. Given the belief that the output/employment costs of reducing inflation would be small, new classical economists see no necessity to follow a policy of gradual monetary contraction and argue that the authorities might just as well announce a dramatic reduction in the rate of monetary expansion in order to reduce inflation to their preferred target rate.

3.5 CONCLUSION

The controversy over whether there exists a long-run trade-off between inflation and unemployment has, as we have seen, important implications for the role and conduct of stabilization policy. Keynesians tend to emphasize the potential role for short-run interventionist stabilization policy. Even if the long-run Phillips curve is vertical, arguments justifying intervention to stabilize the economy in the short run can be made on the grounds of either (i) the long time required for the economy to return to the natural rate of unemployment or (ii) the potential to identify and respond to economic disturbances. In contrast monetarists tend to argue that because of a lack of knowledge of how the economy works, including ignorance of the natural rate, governments should refrain from attempting to stabilize the economy in the short run by aggregate demand management policies in case they make matters worse than better. Instead they argue that policy should be carried out according to rules, the best known of which is that the authorities should pursue a fixed rate of monetary growth in line with the long-run growth potential of the economy. In the next chapter we turn to discuss the role of money in the determination of economic activity.

APPENDIX: ADAPTIVE AND RATIONAL EXPECTATIONS

The difficulty concerning modelling of expectations is that they are internal to the economic agent(s) forming the expectations. They are therefore not directly observable. Two hypotheses have been extensively used in the literature: (i) adaptive expectations and (ii) rational expectations. These are discussed below.

A3.1 Adaptive Expectations

A3.1.1 Nature of adaptive expectations

The main idea behind the adaptive expectations hypothesis (first modelled by Cagan, 1956, in the context of hyperinflation) is that economic agents adapt their expectations in the light of past experience and that they can learn from their mistakes.

More formally adaptive expectations may be represented as follows:

$$\dot{P}^e_t - \dot{P}^e_{t-1} = \alpha\,(\dot{P}_t - \dot{P}^e_{t-1}) \qquad \text{(A3.1)}$$

Equation (A3.1) shows that expectations are revised each period ($\dot{P}^e_t - \dot{P}^e_{t-1}$) by a constant fraction ($0 < \alpha < 1$) of the discrepancy between the current observed value of the variable ($\dot{P}_t$) and the previously made expected value of that variable ($\dot{P}^e_{t-1}$). In other words expectations are revised by a fraction of the last error made ($\dot{P}_t - \dot{P}^e_{t-1}$).

Equation (A3.1) can be rearranged and factorized:

$$\dot{P}^e_t = \alpha\dot{P}_t + (1 - \alpha)\,\dot{P}^e_{t-1} \qquad \text{(A3.2)}$$

If equation (A3.2) is lagged one period:

$$\dot{P}^e_{t-1} = \alpha\dot{P}_{t-1} + (1 - \alpha)\,\dot{P}^e_{t-2} \qquad \text{(A3.3)}$$

Multiplying equation (A3.3) by $(1 - \alpha)$ gives:

$$(1 - \alpha)\, \dot{P}^{e}_{t-1} = \alpha\,(1 - \alpha)\, \dot{P}_{t-1} + (1 - \alpha)^2\, \dot{P}^{e}_{t-2} \qquad \text{(A3.4)}$$

Substituting equation (A3.4) into (A3.2) gives:

$$\dot{P}^{e}_{t} = \alpha \dot{P}_{t} + \alpha(1 - \alpha)\, \dot{P}_{t-1} + (1 - \alpha)^2\, \dot{P}^{e}_{t-2} \qquad \text{(A3.5)}$$

By repeated back substitution:

$$\dot{P}^{e}_{t} = \alpha \dot{P}_{t} + \alpha(1 - \alpha)\, \dot{P}_{t-1} \dots\dots \alpha(1 - \alpha)^n\, \dot{P}_{t-n} \qquad \text{(A3.6)}$$

Equation (A3.6) shows that the expected value of the variable is a geometrically weighted average of past observed values of that variable with greater importance attached to the value of the variable in more recent periods.

The operational advantage of adaptive expectations is that representation of the expectational variable is easily transferred into an observed variable using the so-called 'Koyck' transformation.

Assume:

$$Y_t = \beta\, X^{e}_{t} + \epsilon_t \qquad \text{(A3.7)}$$

where Y represents the dependent variable, X the independent variable, X^{e}_{t} the expected value X will take in period$_t$ and ϵ is a random error term.

From (A3.2):

$$X^{e}_{t} = \alpha X_t + (1 - \alpha)\, X^{e}_{t-1} \qquad \text{(A3.8)}$$

Substituting (A3.8) into (A3.7) produces:

$$Y_t = \alpha\beta X_t + \beta(1 - \alpha)\, X^{e}_{t-1} + \epsilon_t \qquad \text{(A3.9)}$$

Lagging (A3.7) by one period and multiplying by $(1 - \alpha)$ produces:

$$(1 - \alpha) Y_{t-1} = \beta(1 - \alpha)\, X^{e}_{t-1} + (1 - \alpha)\, \epsilon_{t-1} \qquad \text{(A3.10)}$$

Subtracting (A3.10) from (A3.9) gives:

$$Y_t = \alpha\beta X_t + (1 - \alpha)\, Y_{t-1} + \epsilon_t - (1 - \alpha)\, \epsilon_{t-1} \qquad \text{(A3.11)}$$

Note that all variables in (A3.11) are directly observable from the data.

A3.1.2 Problems with adaptive expectations

Adaptive expectations is a very mechanical method of modelling expectations formation about any variable. In this method of modelling expectations economic agents base their expectations of future values of a variable only on past values of the variable concerned. Economic agents are assumed to follow a rule-of-thumb approach so that they never take into consideration other additional information that may become available. This means that unless the variable being predicted is stable for a considerable period of time expectations of it will repeatedly be wrong. For example, if inflation is accelerating, inflation expectations will be biased in a downward direction, i.e. they will continuously underestimate future inflation. This problem results from: (i) the assumption that economic agents only partially adjust their expectations by a fraction of the last error made and (ii) the failure of agents to take into consideration additional information available to them, other than past values of the variable concerned, despite making repeated errors. As we will now discuss, this contrasts with the rational expectations hypothesis which implies that economic agents will not form expectations which are systematically wrong over time, i.e. such expectations are unbiased.

A.3.2 Rational Expectations

A3.2.1 Nature of rational expectations

The main idea behind the rational expectations hypothesis (first discussed by Muth, 1961, in the context of microeconomics) is that in forming expectations about the future value of a variable, rational economic agents will make the best (most efficient) use of all publicly available information about the factors which they believe determine that variable. For example, if economic agents believe that the rate of inflation is determined by the rate of monetary expansion then they will make the best use of all publicly available information on rates of monetary expansion in forming their expectations of future rates of inflation. It is important to emphasize that economic agents will make mistakes in their forecasts. Rational expectations is not the same as perfect foresight. However, what rational expectations does imply is that agents will not form expectations which are systematically wrong over time because if they did they would learn from their mistakes and change the way they formed their expectations, thereby eliminating systematic errors. In other words the hypothesis suggests that economic agents form expectations which are 'essentially the same as the predictions of the relevant economic theory' (Muth 1961).

A3.2.2 Problems with rational expectations

A number of objections have been raised against the rational expectations hypothesis and in what follows we outline two of the more serious. The first concerns the costs of acquiring and processing all publicly available information in order to forecast the future value of a variable. At the outset it is important to emphasize that the hypothesis does not require, as some critics have suggested, that economic agents use 'all' publicly available information. Given the costs (i.e. in time, effort and money) of acquiring and processing information it is unlikely that agents would ever use all publicly available information. What the hypothesis does suggest is that rational economic agents will make the 'best' use of all publicly available information in forming their expectations. In other words economic agents will have an incentive to use information up to the point where the marginal benefit (in terms of improved accuracy of the variable being forecast) equals the marginal cost (in terms of acquiring and processing all publicly available information). For example, given (i) price stability over a period of time and (ii) random fluctuations around the stable price level, the adaptive expectations hypothesis provides a cost-effective method of expectations formation. It is also important to emphasize that the hypothesis does not require, as some critics have also suggested, that all individual agents directly acquire and process available information personally. Economic agents can derive information indirectly from, for example, published forecasts and commentaries in the news media. Given that forecasts frequently differ, the problem then arises of discerning which is the 'correct' view.

The second serious objection to the rational expectations hypothesis concerns the problem of how economic agents acquire knowledge of the 'correct' model. Again it is important to stress that the hypothesis does not require that economic agents actually know the correct model of the economy. As noted earlier, what the hypothesis implies is that rational agents will not form expectations which are systematically wrong over time. In other words expectations will resemble those formed 'as if' agents did not know the correct model, to the extent that they will be unbiased and randomly distributed over time. Critics of the rational expectations hypothesis remain unconvinced by these arguments and suggest that due to problems such as the costs of acquiring and processing all available information and uncertainty over the correct model, it 'is' possible for agents to form expectations which are systematically wrong.

4. Money and Economic Activity

4.1 INTRODUCTION

In this chapter we examine the controversy concerning the role of money in the determination of economic activity. This topic has already been introduced in our survey of mainstream macroeconomic models in Chapter 1 and in this chapter we extend that analysis further. In section 4.2 we carry out the analysis within the framework of the IS-LM model prior to a discussion of the various theories of the determination of the money supply in section 4.3. In section 4.4 we examine the money demand function, and in section 4.5 the transmission mechanism of monetary policy is examined in the light of the various theories of the demand for money discussed in section 4.4. The nature of the empirical evidence on the demand for money is discussed in 4.6 and our conclusions are presented in section 4.7.

4.2 MONETARY POLICY IN THE IS-LM MODEL

In Chapter 1 section 1.2.2 we reviewed how the IS-LM model integrates real and monetary factors in determining aggregate demand and therefore the level of economic activity. Within the model the potential for monetary policy to influence the level of output and employment depends on the relative slopes of the IS and LM curves. Monetary policy will be more effective in influencing aggregate demand: (i) the more interest inelastic is the demand for money (i.e. the steeper is the LM curve) and (ii) the more interest elastic is investment (i.e. the flatter is the IS curve). This is illustrated in Figures 4.1 and 4.2.

Figure 4.1 illustrates the importance of the slope of the LM curve for monetary policy. In Figure 4.1 the economy is initially in equilibrium at an income level of Y_0 (i.e. where both LM^{I}_0 and LM^{II}_0 intersect the IS curve at point A). As is evident from Figure 4.1, a given increase in the money supply is more effective the more interest inelastic is the

Figure 4.1 Monetary expansion and the slope of the LM curve

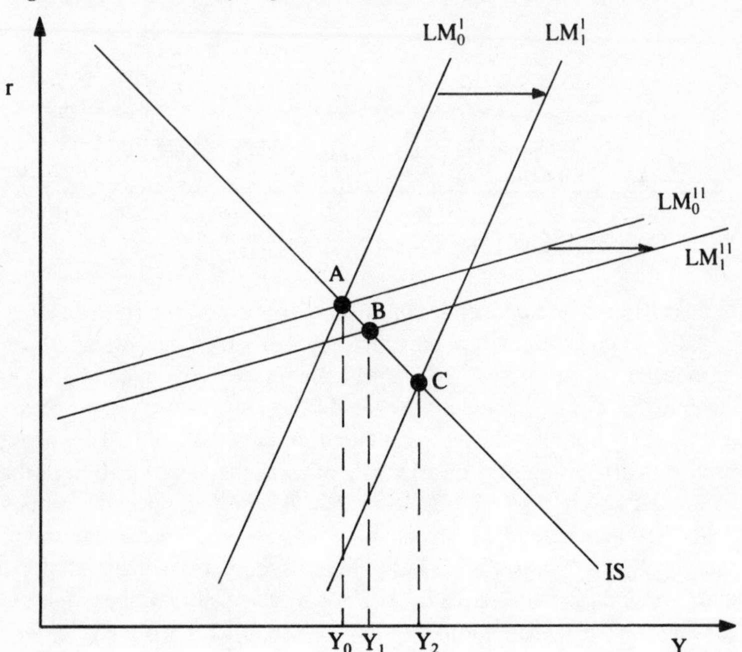

demand for money, i.e. the steeper is the LM curve. This is shown by shifting the curves LM^I_0 and LM^{II}_0 to the right away from the origin by equal horizontal amounts (as indicated by the arrows). In the case of the curve LM^{II} income increases from Y_0 to Y_1 (i.e. LM^{II}_1 intersects the IS curve at point B) whereas in the case of LM^I income increases to a greater extent from Y_0 to Y_2 (i.e. LM^I_1 intersects the IS curve at point C). In the latter case (relatively steep LM curve) income increases and the interest rate falls further than in the former case (relatively flat LM curve) before equilibrium is restored in the money market. It is interesting to note that if the demand for money ever became perfectly elastic with respect to the rate of interest (the extreme Keynesian case of the liquidity trap producing a horizontal LM curve) then monetary policy would be completely ineffective in influencing the level of economic activity.

Figure 4.2 illustrates the importance of the slope of the IS curve for monetary policy. In Figure 4.2 the economy is initially in equilibrium

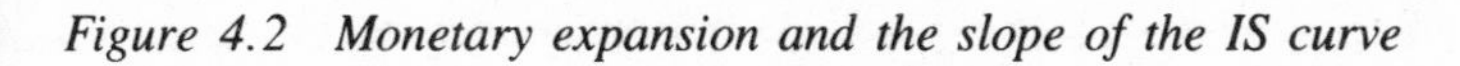

Figure 4.2 Monetary expansion and the slope of the IS curve

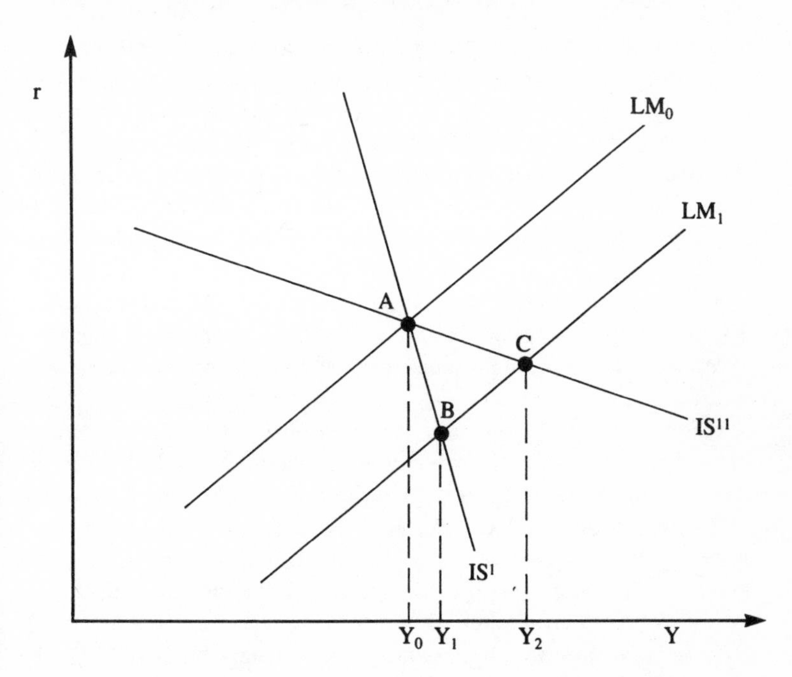

at an income level of Y_0 (i.e. where LM_0 intersects both IS^I and IS^{II} at point A). As is evident from Figure 4.2, a given increase in the money supply which shifts the LM curve from LM_0 to LM_1 is more effective the more interest elastic is investment, i.e. the flatter is the IS curve. In the case of IS^I income increases from Y_0 to Y_1 (i.e. LM_1 intersects IS^I at point B) whereas in the case of IS^{II} income increases from Y_0 to Y_2 (i.e. LM_1 intersects IS^{II} at point C). It is also interesting to note that if investment were perfectly inelastic with respect to the rate of interest (i.e. the extreme Keynesian case of a vertical IS curve) then monetary policy would again be ineffective in influencing the level of output and employment.

Within this framework of analysis the Keynesian position can be characterized by a relatively flat LM curve and a relatively steep IS curve. In this case monetary policy is relatively ineffective in influencing the level of economic activity. In contrast the monetarist position highlighting the effectiveness of monetary policy can be characterized by a relatively steep LM curve and a relatively flat IS curve. Even within the IS-LM framework the foregoing characterization does not do full justice to the monetarist position concerning the effectiveness of monetary policy. An increase in the money supply is likely to cause the IS curve to shift outwards to the right due to substitution of money for real assets as envisaged by Friedman's restatement of the quantity theory of money (see section 4.4.4) thereby further increasing the effectiveness of monetary policy. Finally it is important to note that unlike the Keynesian position the monetarist stance is usually set within the context of an economy operating at or close to full employment (i.e. at the natural rate of unemployment) so that in the long run expansionary monetary policy will not affect output and employment, i.e. money is neutral with respect to real variables.

Accommodation of the new classical position within the IS-LM framework requires the distinction between anticipated and unanticipated monetary shocks. Any anticipated expansionary monetary shock would leave the position of the LM curve unaltered since the anticipated monetary expansion would induce an immediate increase in the price level, which would just offset the increase in the nominal quantity of money so that the real value of the money supply remained unaltered. In contrast, an unanticipated expansionary monetary shock would in the short run have real effects since agents would be misled into thinking that there was a real increase in aggregate demand in line with the analysis presented in Chapter 1, section 1.3.3.

As a means of analysing the role of money in the determination of economic activity the IS-LM analysis is unsatisfactory for a number of reasons. First, the money supply is assumed to be exogenously determined by the authorities. We examine the validity of this assumption in the next section. Secondly, changes in the money supply, it is assumed, work through a 'money-bonds' portfolio adjustment to affect 'the' rate of interest and aggregate demand. In fact in the real world a wide range of financial assets exist, each of which is likely to bear its own rate of interest. This would not be a serious drawback provided all rates of interest moved in line with each other. In practice this does not always appear to be the case. Thirdly, the analysis implicitly assumes that the money demand function is stable. These last two caveats are examined in sections 4.5 and 4.6 respectively.

4.3 THE DETERMINATION OF THE MONEY SUPPLY

4.3.1 The Multiplier Approach

Perhaps the most common explanation of the determination of the money supply is given by the multiplier approach. This comes in a number of guises with varying degrees of complexity, depending on the various assumptions made. In what follows we present a relatively simple model which conveys the essential flavour of this approach. The interested student is referred to the work of Brunner and Meltzer (see, e.g., 1968) for a more sophisticated analysis (and for that matter more complicated algebra).

Initially we assume that the money supply (M) consists of: (i) notes and coins which are held by the non-bank public (H_p) and (ii) bank deposits (D). In this context, notes and coins are termed high-powered money or, alternatively, the monetary base (H) which is held both by the non-bank public and the banks (H_B). Thus:

$$M = H_p + D \tag{4.1}$$

$$H = H_p + H_B \tag{4.2}$$

Two further assumptions are made about the portfolio behaviour of the banks and the non-bank public. It is assumed that the non-bank public maintain holdings of notes and coins in proportion to their holdings of deposits. Similarly, banks are assumed to maintain their holdings of notes and coins in proportion to the total of deposits issued. If these two proportions are denoted α and β respectively, then:

$$H_p = \alpha D \tag{4.3}$$

$$H_B = \beta D \tag{4.4}$$

Substituting (4.3) into (4.1) and rearranging produces:

$$M = (1 + \alpha)D \tag{4.5}$$

Substituting (4.3) and (4.4) into (4.2) and rearranging gives:

$$H = (\alpha + \beta)D \tag{4.6}$$

Substituting for D from (4.6) into (4.5) provides:

$$M = [(1 + \alpha)/(\alpha + \beta)]H \tag{4.7}$$

Equation (4.7) shows the money supply as a function of high-powered money (H) and the portfolio parameters α and β. The term $(1 + \alpha)/(\alpha + \beta)$ is known as the money multiplier and, since α and β are both less than 1, the multiplier has a value in excess of 1 so that an expansion of high-powered money leads to a more than proportionate expansion in the money supply.

The source of high-powered money can be demonstrated using the simple stylized balance sheet of a central bank shown in Table 4.1 in conjunction with the definition of the financing of the public sector deficit (PSD).

Table 4.1: Central bank balance sheet

Liabilities		*Assets*	
Notes and coins	(H)	Loans to the government	(CLG)
Government deposits	(DG)	Foreign exchange reserves	(F)

The liabilities of the central bank comprise notes and coins and government deposits while assets comprise loans to the government and foreign exchange reserves. In order to simplify the analysis we are ignoring bankers' deposits and loans to banks from the liabilities and assets sides of the central bank balance sheet respectively.

The public sector deficit is assumed to be financed by borrowing from the non-bank private sector (PLG) or the banks, both the central bank (CLG) and other banks (BLG), so that:

$$PSD = \Delta\, CLG + \Delta\, PLG + \Delta\, BLG \tag{4.8}$$

where Δ refers to the change in the stock of the asset concerned, i.e. the appropriate flow concept. From the balance sheet presented in Table 4.1:

$$\Delta\, CLG = \Delta\, H + \Delta\, DG - \Delta\, F \tag{4.9}$$

Substituting for Δ CLG in (4.8) from (4.9) and assuming that the government's deposit balance is constant so that Δ DG = 0 gives:

$$PSD = \Delta H + \Delta PLG + \Delta BLG - \Delta F \qquad (4.10)$$

Changes in the stock of high-powered money therefore depend on the size of the public sector deficit, the extent of borrowing by the government from the private sector (including banks) and the volume of intervention in the foreign exchange markets. In other words, changes in the stock of high-powered money depend upon fiscal and monetary policy and the state of the balance of payments. *Ceteris paribus*, the stock of high-powered money is increased by a public sector deficit, and a balance of payments surplus, and reduced by sales of government debt to the private sector.

Combination of the money multiplier (4.7) and the financing of the public sector deficit (4.10) provides a complete explanation of the determination of the money supply. At this stage it is worth noting that our analysis is overly simple in that we have not specified the full menu of financing options open to the government. Nevertheless it is sufficient to demonstrate the general tenor of the approach and to point to the limitations inherent in it.

First, it is not at all apparent that the two portfolio parameters, α and β are constant. In the case of β, most governments impose a minimum reserve ratio on banks and, in practice, banks tend to hold high-powered money balances in excess of this minimum requirement. It would be expected that the precise levels of their holdings would depend on the opportunity cost of holding reserve assets and the returns on alternative assets in addition to the volume of deposits. Similarly the parameter α would depend on the return on high-powered money (normally specified as a convenience yield since the nominal return on notes and coins is zero) relative to returns on alternative assets. Secondly, the holdings of high-powered money by both the banks and the public might be influenced by the composition of the rest of the portfolio. For example, if the banks have a large volume of time deposits for which they know the date of withdrawal, then their requirement to hold reserve assets to meet random withdrawals of deposits will be reduced. Thirdly, changing the assumptions can easily lead to a theory of money determined by the demand for bank loans (so-called credit approach). Intuitively this approach can be explained in the following manner. Assume that: (i) the assets in a bank's balance sheet consist of loans to the public and holdings of notes and coins and (ii) the supply of high-powered money is perfectly elastic because the government chooses to maintain stable interest rates. Then as the demand for loans increases the government will supply high-powered money to maintain the ruling interest rate so that the money supply will expand. This means that the money supply becomes a function of the demand for bank loans.

Both these explanations of the money supply process depend on the assumed behaviour of the government. In the traditional multiplier approach, it is assumed that the government is prepared to let the interest rate fluctuate in response to exogenous changes in the quantity of high-powered money. In contrast, in the credit approach it is the quantity of high-powered money (and therefore the supply of money) which is assumed to fluctuate in response to exogenous changes in the demand for bank credit. In practice, most governments appear to follow a mixture of both policies. Interest rate stability is a prime target in day-to-day operations in the money market but the target rate of interest is varied in response to undesired changes in the money supply.

The most serious of the criticisms refers to the assumption of constant portfolio parameters. Relaxation of this assumption leads to a system of equations describing the portfolio behaviour of the various parties, i.e. the government, the non-bank private sector and the banks. This would include the demand for and supply of bank deposits, the demand for high-powered money as well as the demand for government debt.

4.3.2 The Flow of Funds Approach

A second approach to money supply determination is via the flow of funds. Recall that the money supply can be defined as:

$$M = H_p + D \tag{4.1}$$

and

$$H = H_p + H_B \tag{4.2}$$

We can also define a simple bank's balance sheet as:

$$D = H_B + BLG + BLP \tag{4.11}$$

where BLP is bank lending to the non-bank private sector.

Substituting for H_B from (4.2) in (4.11) produces:

$$D = H - H_p + BLG + BLP \qquad (4.12)$$

Substituting for D in (4.1) from (4.12) gives:

$$M = H + BLG + BLP \qquad (4.13)$$

Taking first differences of (4.13) to change into flow terms produces:

$$\Delta M = \Delta H + \Delta BLG + \Delta BLP \qquad (4.14)$$

From (4.9) (again assuming that $\Delta DG = 0$):

$$\Delta CLG = \Delta H - \Delta F \qquad (4.15)$$

Also from (4.8):

$$\Delta BLG = PSD - \Delta CLG - \Delta PLG \qquad (4.16)$$

Substituting (4.15) and (4.16) into (4.14) provides:

$$\Delta M = PSD - \Delta PLG + \Delta BLP + \Delta F \qquad (4.17)$$

This suggests that the change in the money supply is a function of the size of the public sector deficit less the flow of lending by the non-bank private sector to the public sector plus bank lending to the non-bank private sector plus increases in the central bank's holdings of foreign exchange reserves following intervention in the foreign exchange markets. The term ($PSD - \Delta PLG + \Delta BLP$) is termed domestic credit expansion and this demonstrates that, given intervention in the foreign exchange markets by the authorities, changes in the money supply originate from both domestic and foreign sources.

Determination of the supply of money via the flow of funds is open to the same objections as discussed above with reference to the money multiplier. Equation (4.17) is an identity and tells us nothing about the underlying behavioural relationships and as such represents a mere accounting identity. Consequently an adequate description of the money supply process through the flow of funds approach requires specification of the underlying portfolio behavioural equations.

4.3.3 Concluding Comments

We have completed our survey of the determination of the money supply. Our conclusions are that either of the two approaches discussed above only provide a framework within which the money supply process can be examined. A specification of the underlying portfolio preferences is necessary to provide a full description. One example of a fairly detailed portfolio approach to the determination of the quantity of money is given in Thompson (1988).

Our discussion also sheds some light on the controversy over whether the money supply is exogenous or endogenous. Endogeneity can arise from two sources. The first situation occurs when the government pursues a target other than that of the money supply. Two such cases exist. First, if the government adopts an interest rate policy, then the money supply is

Figure 4.3 Stabilization of the interest rate and the endogeneity of the money supply

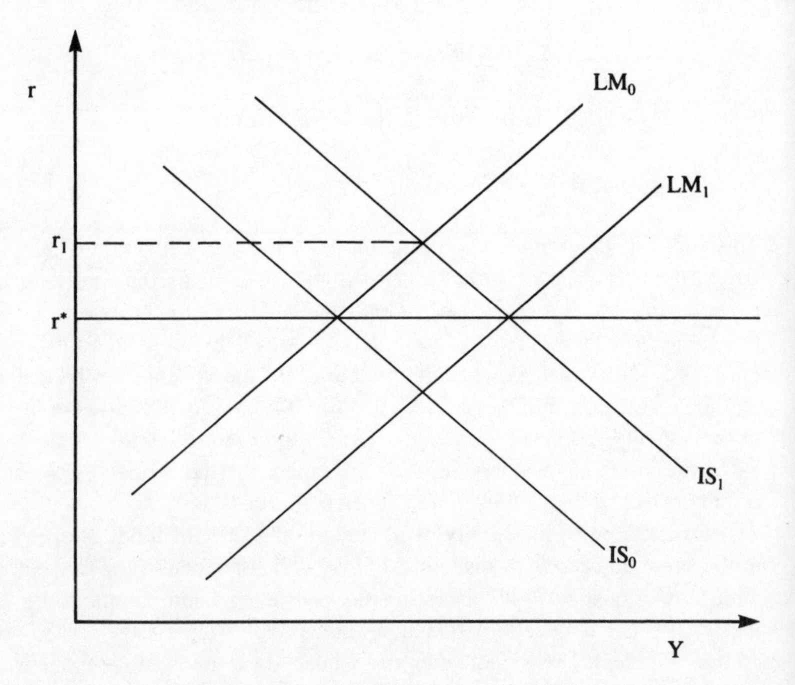

subordinated to interest rate determination and becomes endogenous. This is demonstrated in Figure 4.3. IS_0 and LM_0 represent the original curves with an equilibrium rate of interest equal to r^* which also represents the government's target rate. An expansionary real shock occurs, shifting the IS curve outwards from IS_0 to IS_1 which in the absence of government intervention, causes the rate of interest to rise to r_1. Since r_1 is above r^*, the government intervenes, expanding the money supply so that the LM curve shifts from LM_0 to LM_1. In other words the money supply becomes endogenous. A similar effect arises when the government pursues a target exchange rate. In this case reference to equation (4.17) illustrates the fact that intervention in the foreign exchange markets causes changes in Δ F (the central bank's holdings of foreign currency reserves) so that the money supply becomes endogenous. This exposition entails the assumption that it is very difficult for the authorities to sterilize the effects of foreign exchange intervention. It is interesting to note, however, that these two causes of endogeneity may be obviated by the government avoiding the alternative targets of interest or exchange rates.

The second reason why the money supply may become endogenous is more fundamental. The portfolio behaviour underlying either the multiplier or the flow of funds approach is likely to be, at least partly, endogenous. In the case of the multiplier approach, for example, an increase in the demand for bank loans is likely to lead to an increase in the loan rate of interest and, therefore, a reduction in the quantity of reserves given the level of deposits as banks try to cash in on the more profitable bank lending. Clearly the money supply is partly endogenous and the controversy becomes one of degree and therefore an empirical question of the relative importance of the endogenous and exogenous determinants of the money supply. We now move on to discuss the demand for money.

4.4 THE DEMAND FOR MONEY

In this section we briefly survey traditional theories concerning the demand for money. The brevity of the survey reflects the fact that much of the analysis will be well known to our readers.

4.4.1 The Traditional Quantity Theory of Money

Study of the demand for money is usefully commenced with reference to the early quantity theory of money. Briefly the quantity theory dealt with equilibrium situations where the demand for money was equal to the supply of money, and was therefore an exercise in comparative statics. The fundamental (or Fisher) equation is given by:

$$MV = PT \tag{4.18}$$

where M represents money in equilibrium (i.e. where demand equals supply), V is the transactions velocity of circulation, P is the price per transaction and T the number of transactions. As stated above, the equation is a truism since both sides represent the value of total expenditure. What transforms a truism into a theory is the underlying behavioural assumptions. These were: (i) V was fixed owing to institutional factors, (ii) the money supply was exogenous and (iii) T was fixed because the economy tended towards full employment. Given these assumptions, the price level was held to be proportionate to the money supply, i.e.

$$P = \lambda M \text{ where } \lambda = (V/T) \text{ a constant.} \tag{4.19}$$

This leads to the prediction that an expansion in the money supply only leads to an increase in the price level in the long run.

4.4.2 The Keynesian Approach

The problem with the traditional quantity theory approach is that the velocity of circulation is observed to change at least in the short run. Furthermore, the tendency of the economy towards full employment without government intervention is the subject of much controversy. Keynesian liquidity preference attempted to overcome these problems. The demand for money was divided into three main motives. Holdings of money under the transactions and precautionary motives were held to depend on income. The novel approach was the development of the speculative motive for holding money, with the quantity of money held under this motive being termed idle balances. Money was perceived to be a very close substitute for bonds. Falling interest rates implied rising bond prices. Thus in the circumstances when a speculator expected interest rates to fall he would hold bonds in order to obtain the resulting capital gain. Individual speculators were also assumed to assess the future course of interest rates by comparing the current level with some reference to a perceived normal level. Market holdings of both bonds and money occurred because of different expectations amongst speculators. The higher the current rate of interest the greater the number of speculators expecting future reductions in interest rates (rising bond prices) and the less money demanded, and vice versa. Keynesian analysis gave a special twist to the theory of the demand for money. At very low interest rates, the expectations of speculators would become concentrated. They would believe that the only probable future course of interest rates would be upwards so that the money demand curve would become infinitely elastic. This is the so-called 'liquidity trap' and some Keynesian theorists moved the analysis further by assuming that the liquidity trap was the normal state of events – see the Radcliffe Report (1959) for one example of this belief.

One further modification of the demand for money took the form of suggesting that the transactions demand for money would be interest elastic (Baumol 1952; Tobin 1956). This development merely emphasized the interest elasticity of the demand for money and tended, therefore, towards the Keynesian conclusion that the LM curve was relatively flat. Subsequent progress arose from two differing approaches. First, in the Keynesian tradition, Tobin (1958) put forward a risk aversion theory of the demand for money. Secondly, from a monetarist stance, Friedman restated the quantity theory of money.

4.4.3 Tobin's Risk Aversion Theory of the Demand for Money

Tobin's analysis is interesting because it forms an early attempt to utilize portfolio theory to explain holdings of idle balances of money as a supplement to the speculative motive. The key proposition of risk aversion can easily be demonstrated by considering a simple choice situation. An agent is offered a choice of one of two options:

(i) A certain payment of £100, or
(ii) A payment of £200 or a payment of zero each with the same probability of 0.5.

In the case of both options the expected value is £100. A risk-averse agent would select option (i) because option (ii) involves extra risk in the form of zero payment. A risk-neutral agent would be indifferent between the two options since they offer the same expected payment. A risk lover would select option (ii) because of the chance of payment of £200. If the assumption of risk aversion is made, then the economic agent would accept extra risk only if the expected return is higher. This forms the basis of Tobin's risk aversion approach to the demand for idle balances.

In this analysis the choice facing the individual agent is the allocation of wealth between bonds and money. For ease of exposition money is assumed to earn a zero rate of return in contrast to bonds, which earn a return including expected capital gains. The market price of bonds fluctuates according to market conditions so that there is a risk that their return will be different from that expected – note that the risk envisaged is due to price changes, not default. This risk can be measured by the standard deviation of the returns around their expected value. Money is capital certain and, therefore, involves no risk. The following diagrammatic approach follows Laidler (1985) rather than that adopted by Tobin.

Figure 4.4 Risk and the allocation of wealth between money and bonds

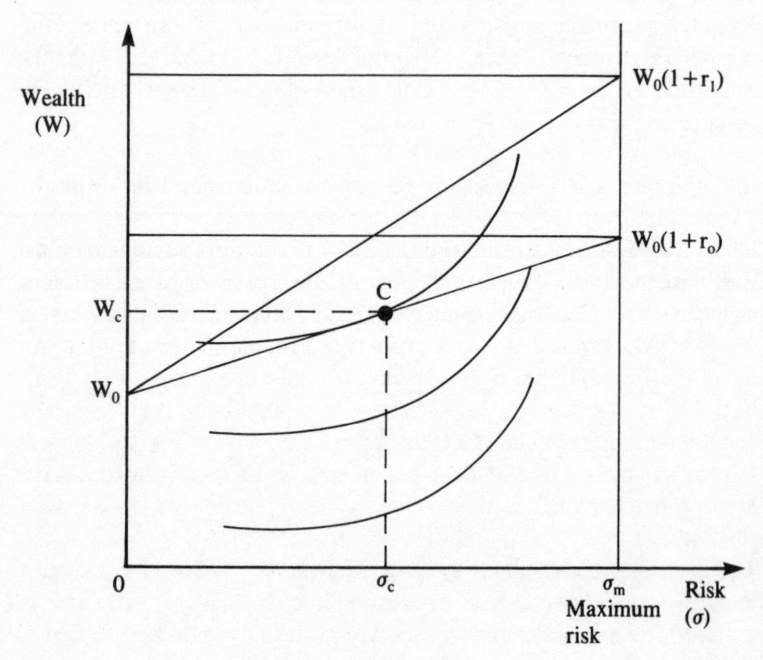

In Figure 4.4 risk (as measured by the standard deviation of the expected returns) and wealth are represented on the horizontal and vertical axes respectively. Wealth is to be allocated between bonds and money so as to maximize utility. If all initial wealth is allocated to bonds, then expected wealth equals $W_0(1 + r_0)$ where r is the expected return on bond and risk will equal σ_m. Conversely, if all initial wealth is allocated to money, expected wealth remains equal to W_0 and risk is equal to zero. Any point along the line W_0 to $W_0(1 + r_0)$ represents a combination of risk and expected wealth afforded by a mix of bond and money holdings. The individual's indifference curves will slope upwards given the assumption of risk aversion. In general, equilibrium for the individual can occur at any point along the line W_0 to $W_0(1 + r_0)$. In Figure 4.4 equilibrium is defined at point C with risk equal to σ_c and expected wealth to equal W_c. An increase in the expected return to bonds will rotate the line W_0 to $W_0(1 + r_0)$ anticlockwise to W_0 to $W_0(1 + r_1)$. This is likely to increase the individual holdings of bonds and reduce that of money. This is not certain, however. As in all cases of indifference curve analysis it depends on the relative strength of the substitution and income (or in this case wealth) effects. The substitution effect will always cause bonds to be substituted for money as interest rates rise. The wealth effect may, however, lead to either a reduction or an increase in bond holdings and the overall effect depends on the combination of these two effects.

In principle, Tobin's analysis is easily extended to more than two assets. The two key motives in the allocation of wealth between the competing assets are (i) expected return and (ii) risk as represented by the mean and standard deviation or variance of the probability distributions associated with the possible outcomes. For obvious reasons this is known as the mean-variance approach to portfolio modelling. In practice considerable difficulties arise with describing portfolio decision-making by graphical methods if more than two assets are involved. So recourse has to be made to more formal methods of obtaining exact or approximate solutions to a number of equations representing the demand for various assets. These methods are beyond the scope of this text but for one such example of a series of portfolio demand equations for the non-bank private sector the interested reader is again referred to Thompson (1988).

4.4.4 Friedman's Restatement of the Quantity Theory of Money

Tobin's analysis is based firmly in the Keynesian tradition since substitutes for money are restricted to financial assets. In contrast, Friedman's (1956) restatement of the quantity theory broadens the range of substitutes to include real assets. For Friedman, the demand for money can be analysed in the same way as the demand for a durable good. Durable goods provide a flow of services from which ultimate wealth holders derive utility. It is asserted that money also yields a flow of services (hence utility) to the holder and consequently money is treated as an asset, with the demand for money analysed as a demand for a stock. The demand for money (like the demand for any asset) depends on the wealth constraint (determining the maximum amount of money that can be held) and the return on money in relation to the return on other assets in which wealth can be held. In the latter case Friedman distinguished five forms in which wealth could be held: money, bonds, equities, physical goods and human capital. The way total wealth is allocated between the various forms depends upon the relative rates of return on the various assets. Friedman broadened the concept of wealth to include human (discounted future labour income) and non-human wealth. Since wealth is difficult to measure empirically, permanent income was used as a proxy for wealth. A further qualification is placed on the role of wealth as the constraint on the maximum amount of money that can be held. In the absence of slavery, trade in human wealth is restricted to borrowing on the strength of future income and investing in methods to increase future earning capacity. In view of the difficulty of substituting human for non-human wealth, Friedman suggested that the ratio of human to non-human wealth should be included in the specification of the demand for money function.

As noted above, the range of assets incorporated in the demand function is wider than that envisaged by Keynesians and incorporates real as well as financial assets. Relative returns on the various assets take the place of relative prices in traditional consumer theory. For bonds and equities these are defined as expected income plus expected capital gains. For money itself the return comprises a return in kind (owing to the services that are derived from holding it) plus a real return (which can be positive or negative) depending on movements in the price level, given that money is perceived by Friedman as a temporary abode of purchasing power. In the case of real assets a flow of returns is generated but these rates are not always obviously observable in the market-place.

Within this analysis holders of money will adjust their holdings of money balances if the rate of return on other forms in which wealth can be held should change. The analysis therefore predicts that the demand for money will fall, *ceteris paribus*, if the return on other assets rises, and vice versa. Individuals will allocate wealth between the different assets to equalize marginal rates of return, thereby maximizing their utility. If marginal rates of return are not equal, a reallocation of wealth between assets would take place. In other words equilibrium in the portfolio of wealth exists where the returns are such that all the assets are willingly held. As we shall discuss in section 4.5.2, this portfolio adjustment process is central to the monetarist approach to the transmission mechanism.

We now turn to consider the mechanism whereby changes in the stock of money affect economic activity.

4.5 THE TRANSMISSION MECHANISM

The transmission mechanism describes the precise way in which changes in the stock of money affect the real sector. Clearly the perception of this mechanism will vary according to the components of the demand for money function.

4.5.1 Keynesian Approach

In Keynesian analysis the transmission mechanism is via the interest rate. An increase in the supply of money will drive the rate of interest down so that the money supply is willingly held. The lower rate of interest will increase the net present value of future streams of income arising from investment projects above their supply price and result in an increase in investment. This analysis may be presented more formally. Assume that firms finance investment by way of retained earnings and new issues of equity. In this case, the market value of a firm's equity is given by the discounted value of the future dividends (see the note at the end of the chapter) accruing to equity holders so that:

$$V_t = R_t + \frac{R_{t+1}}{(1 + r_e)} + \frac{R_{t+2}}{(1 + r_e)^2} + \ldots \qquad (4.20)$$

where R represents the expected dividend, t the time period and r_e the rate of return required by asset holders to persuade them to hold the equity. For ease of exposition it is convenient to assume that the Rs are constant so that:

$$V_t = R/r_e \qquad (4.21)$$

The replacement cost of the outstanding capital stock is given by P_kK where K is the number of physical units of capital stock and P_k the price per unit. Given the replacement cost of capital and the expected returns the marginal efficiency of capital (ρ_k) is obtained by solving:

$$P_kK = R_t + \frac{R_{t+1}}{(1 + \rho_k)} + \frac{R_{t+2}}{(1 + \rho_k)^2} \quad \ldots \tag{4.22}$$

Equation (4.22) can be simplified in the same way as applied to (4.20) so that:

$$P_kK = R/\rho_k \tag{4.23}$$

The firm will invest in situations where the marginal efficiency of capital is greater than the cost of capital to firms as represented by the return required by equity holders r_e or equivalently investment depends on the ratio (q) of the market valuation of equity to the replacement cost of capital. This is demonstrated in (4.24):

$$q = \rho_k/r_e = V_t/P_kK \tag{4.24}$$

In equilibrium q = 1 so that the marginal efficiency of capital is equal to the return required by shareholders. The greater the positive gap between q and 1, the more new investment will be undertaken. Changes in the value of q can occur through changes in either the price of capital goods, (P_k), which will alter the marginal efficiency of capital, or the required rate of return by equity holders r_e. The transmission mechanism envisaged in this approach is that r_e will itself respond to changes in interest rates generating an increase in aggregate demand.

Where q is greater than 1, an increase in the demand for investment goods (a flow) occurs. The resultant increase in aggregate demand has a 'multiplier' impact on national income, which is eventually likely to cause rising prices. The combination of increases in real income and rising prices will induce a rise in the rate of interest which will, at least partially if not completely, offset the initial fall. The adjustment process is one which is characterized by equilibrium in the money market (attained by way of interest rate changes) accompanied by disequilibrium in other markets. This contrasts with the 'buffer stock' approach discussed later in this section.

Extension of this mechanism to the more general portfolio model within the Keynesian approach modifies the transmission mechanism to some extent. First, the impact of a change in the quantity of money will be diffused since other assets within the portfolio will adjust in response to the shock. This suggests that the impact on aggregate demand will be reduced and that a more appropriate strategy may be to search out and control a group of assets which are close substitutes for each other but poor substitutes for the other assets contained in the portfolio. It is interesting to note that this does not automatically rule out the monetarist approach, since monetarists would argue that money itself is a poor substitute for any particular asset but that the number of potential substitutes is large. Secondly, changes in any one of the other assets (not just money) will also affect aggregate demand because of the diffused effect on the other asset returns within the portfolio.

The Keynesian approach envisages money as a direct substitute for financial assets alone. This may well be overly restrictive as it forces the transmission mechanism to operate via interest changes affecting the interest-elastic components of aggregate demand. A two-stage process is envisaged whereby money affects the rate of interest and the rate of interest affects aggregate demand. As we shall now discuss, the transmission mechanism implicit in Friedman's restatement of the quantity theory is much broader. Monetarists stress a much broader range of assets (financial and real) and associated expenditures than do Keynesians and in consequence attribute a much stronger effect on aggregate spending to monetary impulses.

4.5.2 Monetarist Approach

Earlier, in section 4.4.4, we outlined how in Friedman's restatement of the quantity theory the demand for money depends upon wealth and the return on money in relation to the return on other assets (financial and real) in which wealth can be held. Assuming an initial equilibrium position where wealth is allocated between real and financial assets such that marginal rates of return are equal, we now examine the effect of an increase in the money supply. As the marginal return on any asset diminishes as holdings of it increase, the marginal rate of return on money holdings relative to other assets will fall following an increase in the money supply. In order to bring marginal rates of return back into equilibrium a reallocation of wealth will take place between assets, which will involve alterations of stocks of real as well as financial assets. As excess money balances are exchanged for financial and real assets (such as durable consumer goods and physical capital) their prices will be bid up (i.e. returns on assets are bid down) until portfolio equilibrium is re-established so that once again all assets are willingly held. This portfolio adjustment process then impinges on a wide array of assets and as a result, either directly or indirectly, spending will increase on a wide range of goods and services. However, with the economy operating at or close to full employment increased expenditure generates increases in the price level and real interest rates and output are unaffected in the long run (see, for example, Friedman 1968). In other words money is neutral in the long run. This monetarist transmission mechanism is essentially the same as that discussed in Chapter 3 for the vertical long-run Phillips curve at the natural rate of unemployment.

At this stage of the analysis it is worth returning to the new classical view of the economy. The impact of an increase in the supply of money depends on whether or not the increase is expected. In the case of an anticipated positive monetary shock, the impact will be purely on prices and the change in prices will be instantaneous. Money is, therefore, held to be neutral in both the short and long run if the expansion is anticipated. In the case of an unanticipated monetary shock the transmission mechanism is similar to that discussed above for Friedman. Real activity will temporarily increase but eventually the impact will be entirely taken up by a rise in prices.

4.5.3 The Buffer Stock Approach

Finally in this section we examine the 'buffer stock' approach to the role of money. The essence of this approach is that the demand for money is not directed towards a precise quantity of money which the agent will wish to hold at every point of time but rather towards an average or target value over a period of time. A useful analogy is the role of inventories acting as a shock absorber for changes in demand. In a similar manner money will act as a shock absorber for economic disturbances. Consequently within this approach it is possible from time to time for an agent to be off his demand for money function in the short run without immediately taking offsetting action. Laidler (1990) argues that such a situation is inherent in a market economy where there is no Walrasian auctioneer ensuring that market clearing always exists. In modern economies the normal practice is for goods to be changed for money and subsequently money for goods. Direct barter or instantaneous exchange is of very limited practical use. Money has then a particular advantage in that it can be exchanged for goods without delay. Holdings of an acceptable medium of exchange (i.e. money) prevent surprises in the market, preventing an agent from carrying out his planned buying or selling activities. Buffer stocks of money holdings may, therefore, be a substitute for increased information. The costs of using money as a buffer are connected with changes in the purchasing power of money, that is changes in the average price level. If high and/or variable rates of inflation exist there is a strong incentive for agents to economize on money balances and seek alternative methods of protecting themselves against shocks. One such method is to increase expenditure on seeking out more information. This suggests a transmission mechanism similar to that envisaged in the monetarist approach. Changes in money holdings would affect a wide range of assets, financial and real. As for the monetarist approach, eventually prices would rise but there would be long lags throughout the process as the initial impact would be absorbed by changes in money balances via the buffer stock function and then in aggregate demand. This contrasts with the position of both Keynesians and new classical economists. As we noted earlier, the former argue that the ratee of interest adjusts to ensure that the economy is always on its demand for money function. The latter postulates an instantaneous adjustment to anticipated monetary changes.

Clearly the exact nature of the transmission mechanism is contentious. It may be thought that empirical evidence may throw some light on these matters and provide an indication of which stance is more likely to be correct. This is the subject of the next section, in which we consider evidence on the stability of the demand for money function.

4.6 EMPIRICAL EVIDENCE ON THE DEMAND FOR MONEY

In this section we provide the general flavour of empirical studies rather than precise details of individual studies. The interested reader who wishes to obtain more information on individual studies is referred to the good summaries contained in Laidler (1985) and Stevenson *et al.* (1988).

Early studies of the demand for money have taken the general form:

$$m = \beta_0 + \beta_1 y + \beta_2 p + \beta_3 r \qquad (4.25)$$

All variables are in logarithms with m representing money, y real income, p the general price level and r an appropriate interest rate. Usually β_2 was constrained to equal 1 so that the dependent variable in (4.25) became the real quantity of money $(m-p)$. A further refinement concerned the addition of the lagged dependent variable $(m-p)_{t-1}$ to the variables on the left-hand side of (4.25). This was justified on the grounds of partial adjustment which in turn may be derived from the minimization of a quadratic loss function – for an explanation of these points see any standard text on econometrics, such as Kmenta (1986). Annual and quarterly data were used and the standard result was that both income and the rate of interest were significant determinants of the quantity of money demanded. The money demand function appeared to be stable.

The 1970s produced problems for estimates of the demand for money. Previously stable relationships appeared to break down and the incorporation of additional variables seemed to proffer little help. One possible explanation lies in the assumption that equations of the general form of (4.25) implicitly assume that the observed quantity of money represents the quantity demanded. The buffer stock approach refutes this assumption, suggesting that it is only in the long run that agents will be on their demand for money function. Within this body of theory it is also possible that even in the long run the observed demand for money function will appear to be unstable. This can occur not only because the individual coefficients of the money demand equation change but also because the demand curve itself shifts due to changes in other exogenous variables such as financial innovation. Some support for this proposal is contained in a Bank of England paper by Hall, Henry and Wilcox (1989) using the method of co-integration discussed below. These additional exogenous variables take the form of financial innovation and the development of interest bearing accounts at the narrow money end and wealth effects at the broad end.

The late 1970s and 1980s have seen significant developments in methods of empirical analysis, at least two of which are highly pertinent to the assessment of the early empirical studies of the demand for money. The first of these concerns the development of the error correction method pioneered by Hendry and his associates. At the simplest level the specification of an equation may take the following general form:

$$\Delta Y_t = \beta_0 + \beta_1 \Delta Z_t - \beta_2 (Y/X)_{t-1} \tag{4.26}$$

where Z and X are vectors of relevant variables. Because long-run static equilibrium requires Δ Y and Δ Z to equal 0, it follows that:

$$Y = \beta_0/\beta_2(X) \tag{4.27}$$

This permits the specification of the long-run equilibrium variables, for which economic theory provides good guidance, leaving short-run dynamics, for which economic theory provides little guidance, to be estimated from the data. Hendry and Mizon (1978) used this approach to estimate a demand for money function which incorporated the customary variables, i.e. real money balances, real income and interest rates. The precise model selection procedure used the 'general to specific' approach. This entails specifying a very general model and testing downwards using statistical tests for any constraints imposed, such that specific parameters are zero. The resulting estimated model is then said to be 'data acceptable'.

Further refinement in econometric methods was developed within the framework of 'co-integration'. Whilst detailed explanation of such methods is outside the scope of this text, a general survey will enable the reader to appreciate the problems inherent in the early studies. More detailed expositions are contained in a number of texts, for example Holden, Peel and Thompson (1991). The underlying rationale of the co-integration literature is that regression between variables is a misleading procedure unless the variables themselves are 'stationary', by which it is usually meant that their means and variances are constant over the estimation period. One simple example of this danger is the ease with which it is possible to find reasonable relationships between unconnected variables which are subject to common time trends, the so-called 'spurious regression' problem. If a satisfactory relationship between two or more variables is found by regression methods, and the errors (i.e. actual value minus the value predicted by the regression equation) are stationary then they are said to be 'co-integrated'. A further development within this framework was the Engle and Granger 'two-step' approach. This enables the estimation of the long-term or equilibrium relationship by the method of ordinary least squares and subsequently estimating the dynamic or short-run relationship from the residuals of the long-run estimates. This was the approach used by Hall, Henry and Wilcox (1989), who purport to find stable demand functions for M0, M1, M3 and M4 for the UK over differing periods varying between 1963 and 1987. As noted earlier, additional variables were necessary to derive these relationships, which is perhaps not surprising given the degree of financial innovation over this period.

The development of these new econometric methods also offers a suggested reason for the breakdown of the money demand functions estimated by the more traditional methods. This is that the estimates were incorrect, and not the underlying function. Of course, only time will tell if these newer estimation methods are more robust.

4.7 CONCLUSION

In this chapter we have surveyed the role money plays in the determination of real income. A wide variety of views of this role have been identified in our discussion, varying from the extreme Keynesian view that money has no effect on real or nominal variables to the standard monetarist view that money is 'neutral' (i.e. not affecting real variables) in the long run. The new classical view is rather different, since the distinction between anticipated and unanticipated monetary shocks is introduced with only the latter affecting real output and then only in the short run. The question of the endogeneity of the money supply is also contentious.

In view of these disagreements, we surveyed the empirical literature to see if a firm conclusion could be drawn regarding which view is most likely to be correct. Unfortunately the situation has not been clarified. All sides in the dispute can find empirical evidence to confirm their belief in the importance of money but not to a level adequate to convince proponents of the opposing view. The following quotation from Fair (1979) may still represent the difficulties inherent in empirical studies: 'It is an unfortunate characteristic of macroeconomic models that the coefficients can change substantially as the sample period changes.' We now turn to consider the controversy over the potency of fiscal policy.

NOTE

By definition the expected rate of return on an equity (r_e) can be defined as:

$$r_e = (E_tP_{t+1} + E_tD_t - P_t)/P_t \tag{4.28}$$

where P equals the price of the share, D is the dividend and E refers to the expectation operator.

Solving (4.28) for P_t and noting that in equilibrium the required rate of return is equal to the required rate of discount:

$$P_t = (E_tP_{t+1} + E_tD_t)/(1 + r_e) \qquad (4.29)$$

In a similar way the forecast of price in period t+1 is given by:

$$E_tP_{t+1} = (E_tP_{t+2} + E_tD_{t+1})/(1 + r_e) \qquad (4.30)$$

Successive substitution for P_{t+1} provides the following explanation of the share price purely in terms of dividends, given that the discounted value of the ultimate price term tends to zero as i tends to infinity.

This supports the formula given in (4.20) where V is the price of the equity and R is the dividend represented by P and D in (4.29) above.

5. Fiscal Policy and Aggregate Demand

5.1 INTRODUCTION

The aim of this chapter is to examine the role of fiscal policy in the light of the Keynesian–monetarist debate over whether fiscal policy matters. Fiscal policy can be defined as any measure which alters government expenditure and/or tax payments for the purpose of influencing aggregate demand. Views concerning the power of fiscal policy to influence real income and output have changed dramatically over recent decades. Initially, in section 5.2, we look at the orthodox Keynesian view that fiscal policy matters. In section 5.3 we examine the typical monetarist view that in the long run fiscal policy has no real impact on the economy and merely changes the composition of national income. Subsequently, in section 5.4, we discuss what effect the introduction of the government budget constraint into the analysis has on the predictions of the power of fiscal policy. Having discussed the analysis in terms of the familiar IS-LM model of a closed economy in sections 5.2–5.4, in section 5.5 we consider the issue of whether fiscal policy matters in the context of the AD-AS model. Finally, in section 5.6 we draw together some conclusions concerning the controversy over the potency of fiscal policy.

5.2 KEYNESIAN VIEW

5.2.1 Fiscal Policy and the Relative Slopes of the IS and LM Curves

The Keynesian view that fiscal policy matters and can be used to influence aggregate demand and produce changes in real income can be analysed in the context of the IS-LM model of a closed economy. Within the model the potential for fiscal policy to influence the level of output and employment depends on the relative slopes of the IS and LM curves.

Fiscal policy will be more effective in influencing aggregate demand: (i) the more interest elastic is the demand for money (i.e. the flatter is the LM curve) and (ii) the less interest elastic is investment (i.e. the steeper is the IS curve). This is illustrated in Figures 5.1 and 5.2.

Figure 5.1 Fiscal expansion and the slope of the LM curve

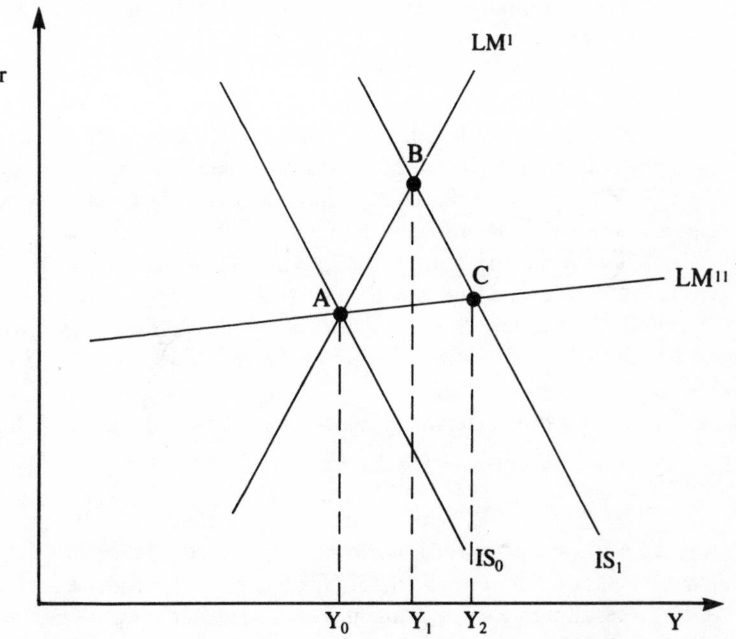

Figure 5.1 illustrates the importance of the slope of the LM curve for fiscal policy. In Figure 5.1 the economy is initially in equilibrium at an income level of Y_0 (i.e. where IS_0 intersects both LM^I and LM^{II} at point A). As is evident from Figure 5.1 a given fiscal expansion (e.g. an increase in government expenditure) which shifts the IS curve from IS_0 to IS_1 is more effective the more interest elastic is the demand for money (i.e. the flatter is the LM curve). As spending and income increases the transactions demand for money increases and with a fixed money supply results in an increase in the rate of interest. How far the rate of interest increases depends on the interest elasticity of the demand

for money (the slope of the LM curve). The rise in the rate of interest in turn leads to a reduction in private sector investment spending. The flatter (steeper) the LM curve is the less (more) the interest rate increases and the less (more) private sector investment spending will be reduced or crowded out by a rise in government expenditure and in consequence the greater (smaller) is the multiplier effect on income. In the case of the curve LM^{II} income increases from Y_0 to Y_2 (i.e. IS_1 intersects LM^{II} at point C), whereas in the case of LM^{I} income increases to a lesser extent from Y_0 to Y_1 (i.e. IS_1 intersects LM^{I} at point B). The reader should be aware of the two extreme cases of a vertical LM curve (the so-called classical range where the demand for money is perfectly inelastic with respect to the rate of interest) and a horizontal LM curve (the so-called liquidity trap where the demand for money is perfectly elastic with respect to the rate of interest). In the former case fiscal expansion will have no effect on income, as the increase in the rate of interest will reduce private investment by an amount identical to the increase in government expenditure (see Figure 5.4), while in the latter case fiscal expansion will result in the full multiplier effect of the simple Keynesian 45° or cross model.

Figure 5.2 illustrates the importance of the slope of the IS curve for fiscal policy. In Figure 5.2 the economy is initially in equilibrium at an income level of Y_0 (i.e. both IS^{I}_0 and IS^{II}_0 intersect the LM curve at point A). A given fiscal expansion shifts both IS curves to the right away from the origin by equal horizontal amounts (as indicated by the arrows). As is evident from Figure 5.2 fiscal expansion is more effective the less interest-elastic is investment (i.e. the steeper is the IS curve). In the case of the curve IS^{I} income increases from Y_0 to Y_2 (i.e. IS^{I}_1 intersects the LM curve at point C) whereas in the case of IS^{II} income increases to a lesser extent from Y_0 to Y_1 (i.e. IS^{II}_1 intersects the LM curve at point B). It is interesting to note that if investment were perfectly elastic with respect to the rate of interest the IS curve would be horizontal and fiscal policy would be unable to alter the position of the curve. In other words, in this extreme theoretical case fiscal expansion could not alter the rate of interest because an infinitesimally small change in the rate of interest would produce a reduction in private investment equal in magnitude to the increase in government expenditure.

5.2.2 Bond-financed and Money-financed Fiscal Expansion

So far no mention has been made of the way in which expansionary fiscal

Figure 5.2 Fiscal expansion and the slope of the IS curve

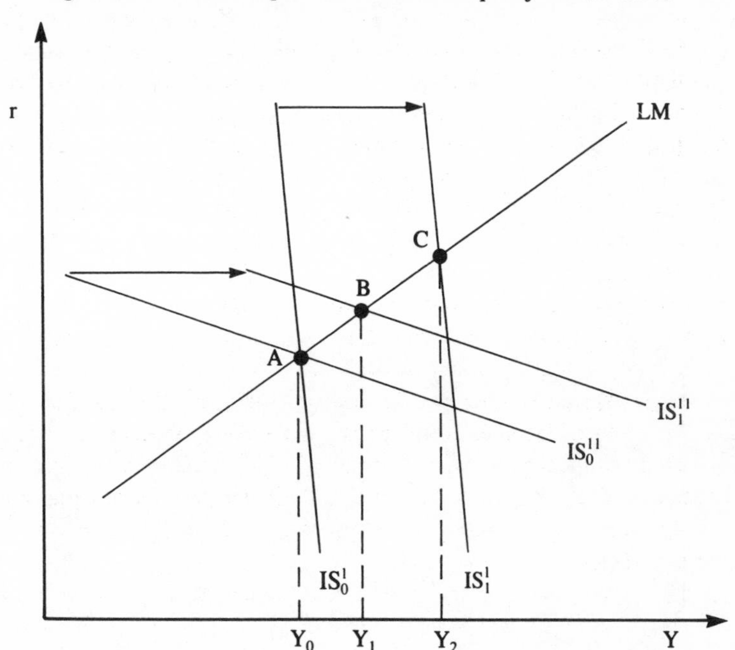

policy may be financed. In a closed economy fiscal expansion in the form of an increase in government expenditure may be financed by an increase in taxes; the sale of bonds; or by an increase in the money stock. Leaving aside the case of a tax-financed increase in government expenditure (i.e. the balanced-budget multiplier) it is apparent that within the Keynesian IS-LM model money-financed fiscal expansion will have a greater impact on income than a bond-financed increase in government expenditure. This is illustrated in Figure 5.3. The economy is initially in equilibrium at an income level of Y_0 (i.e. the intersection of IS_0 and LM_0). In the case of bond-financed fiscal expansion the government borrows from the public by selling bonds and the money is then used by the government to finance its increased expenditure so that the money supply remains unchanged. Bond-financed fiscal expansion shifts the IS curve to the right from IS_0 to IS_1 and results in an increase in income from Y_0 to Y_1 (i.e. the intersection of IS_1 and LM_0). In the case of money-financed fiscal expansion the LM curve also shifts from LM_0 to LM_1 and results in a greater increase in income from Y_0 to Y_2 (i.e. the intersection of LM_1 and IS_1). The reason for this is that the increase in the money supply offsets the positive effect of increased spending and income on the rate of interest and in consequence offsets the crowding out of private sector investment.

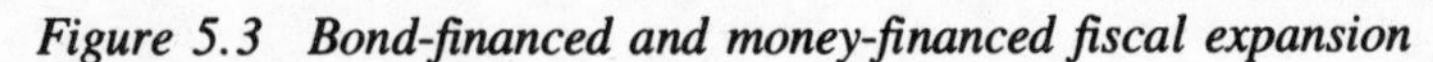

Figure 5.3 Bond-financed and money-financed fiscal expansion

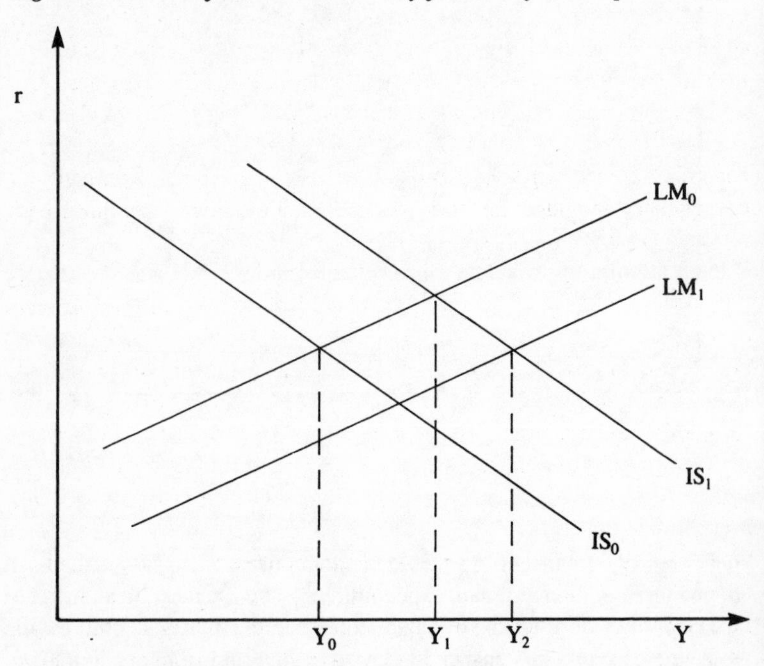

5.2.3 Problem of Measuring the Stance of Fiscal Policy

Before turning to discuss the monetarist view concerning fiscal policy it is worth mentioning the problem of measuring the stance (i.e. restrictive or stimulative) of fiscal policy. The essence of the Keynesian approach is that fiscal policy matters and that by budget manipulation governments can influence aggregate demand in an attempt to stabilize the level of economic activity. In planning policy some measure is therefore needed to indicate the stance and impact of a particular budget programme on the economy.

Let us begin by considering the use of the budget balance to measure whether policy is having an expansionary or contractionary effect on the economy. The relationship between government expenditure and tax revenue is reflected in the position of the budget, which will be in deficit (surplus) where tax revenue is less than (greater than) expenditure. The actual size of the budget deficit/surplus depends partly on the level of economic activity, i.e. the budget position is endogenous to the level of income. A given change in the actual budget deficit/surplus over time may be the result of: (i) planned or discretionary policy changes (e.g. a planned increase in government expenditure) and/or (ii) unplanned, automatic or non-discretionary changes due to changes in the level of economic activity (e.g. tax receipts increase as income increases). In consequence the budget position is an unreliable guide to the direction of fiscal policy.

In an attempt to provide a more reliable guide to the stance of fiscal policy the concept of the full employment budget deficit/surplus has been developed. Given a particular fiscal programme the full employment budget position measures what tax receipts and expenditure would be if the economy were at full employment. In so doing it attempts to distinguish the influence of the budget on the economy (i.e. due to discretionary policy changes) from that of the economy on the budget (i.e. due to automatic changes). The full employment budget deficit/surplus indicates whether fiscal policy is stimulative/restrictive while its size indicates the degree of stimulus/restraint being exerted on the economy. Planned fiscal policy changes that increase (reduce) the full employment budget deficit (surplus) either through increased government expenditure and/or reduced taxation indicate an expansionary fiscal policy. In contrast planned changes that reduce (increase) the full employment deficit (surplus) by decreasing expenditure and/or increasing taxation indicate a contractionary policy stance.

At this stage it is interesting to note three additional points with regard to the full employment budget deficit/surplus. First, while this measure gives a more reliable guide (compared to the budget position) to the stance of fiscal policy it is difficult in practice to calculate the full employment budget deficit/surplus. Secondly, in discussing the impact of a particular budget programme on the economy account has to be taken of the fact that different types of taxation and expenditure have different multiplier effects on the level of economic activity. At its simplest an increase in government expenditure will have a greater impact on the economy than a rise in tax payments of the same amount. It is possible therefore for discretionary policy changes to leave the full employment budget position unchanged and still have a positive influence on the level of economic activity, the so-called balanced budget multiplier. For this reason the weighted full employment budget position has been advocated (where the weights measure the relative impact of different types of expenditure and taxation) as a more reliable guide to the impact of a particular budget programme on the economy. This is also subject to the practical measurement problem discussed above. Finally, even when no discretionary fiscal policy changes are introduced automatic changes in the full employment budget position can occur because of economic growth and price inflation. For example, in an economy experiencing inflation real tax receipts will increase due to a progressive tax system denominated in nominal terms. Such automatic changes are commonly referred to as fiscal drag because they act as a drag on the expansion of output and employment.

We now turn to discuss the monetarist view that in the long run fiscal policy has no real impact on the economy.

5.3 MONETARIST VIEW

5.3.1 Nature of Crowding Out

The typical monetarist view concerning fiscal policy is that while 'pure' fiscal expansion (i.e. without accommodating monetary expansion) will influence national income in the short run, in the long run it will crowd out or replace some components of private expenditure so that real income remains unchanged. Complete crowding out occurs where the reduction in private expenditure is identical in magnitude to the increase in government expenditure so that the long-run fiscal multiplier will be zero. Crowding out will be partial if income rises by an amount less than the increase in government expenditure and in this case the value of the multiplier will be between zero and unity. Income could also rise by an amount more than the increase in government expenditure (i.e. giving a multiplier greater than unity) with partial crowding out occurring in *some* areas, for example private investment. Finally, super or over-crowding out arises where the fall in private expenditure is greater than the rise in government expenditure, in which case the multiplier will be negative.

Crowding out itself may be either direct or indirect. Direct crowding out arises where government expenditures provide goods and services which would otherwise have been produced in the private sector, e.g. if the government provides free health care private expenditure on health care will be reduced. In other words, in some areas government and private expenditure are direct substitutes. As direct crowding out is primarily a microeconomic issue it is not pursued further in this chapter. Instead we concentrate on the controversy surrounding indirect crowding out. At the outset the reader should note that, while we will discuss separately the four main reasons advanced in the literature as to why indirect crowding out may occur, these cases are not necessarily mutually exclusive.

5.3.2 Indirect Crowding Out

Indirect crowding out may arise due to the effect of a change in: (i) the interest rate; (ii) wealth; (iii) expectations; and (iv) the price level.

The interest rate effect

We have already discussed, in section 5.2.1, how following an increase in government expenditure (financed by an increase in bonds) the interest rate will rise, which in turn will crowd out or reduce a certain amount of private sector investment. With a vertical LM curve private sector investment will be reduced by exactly the same amount as government expenditure is increased, resulting in complete crowding out and a government expenditure multiplier of zero. Reference to Figure 5.4 reveals that in this case the rate of interest increases from r_0 to r_2 and income remains unchanged at Y_0. With a positively sloped LM curve there will be some partial crowding out of private sector investment following an increase in government expenditure. Reference to Figure 5.4 reveals that in this case the interest rate increases from r_0 to r_1 and income increases from Y_0 to Y_1. While the multiplier is positive it could be less than or greater than unity. What is apparent is that in both cases (i.e. a vertical and a positively sloped LM curve) crowding out of private sector investment occurs due to the interest rate effect so the multipliers are less than the simple Keynesian multiplier that arises in the liquidity trap. In the latter case income would increase from Y_0 to Y_2 because with a constant interest rate at r_0 (see Figure 5.4) no private sector investment is crowded out.

Monetarists accept that the LM curve is not vertical and do not use this extreme case as justification for their belief in complete crowding

Figure 5.4 Crowding out and the interest rate effect

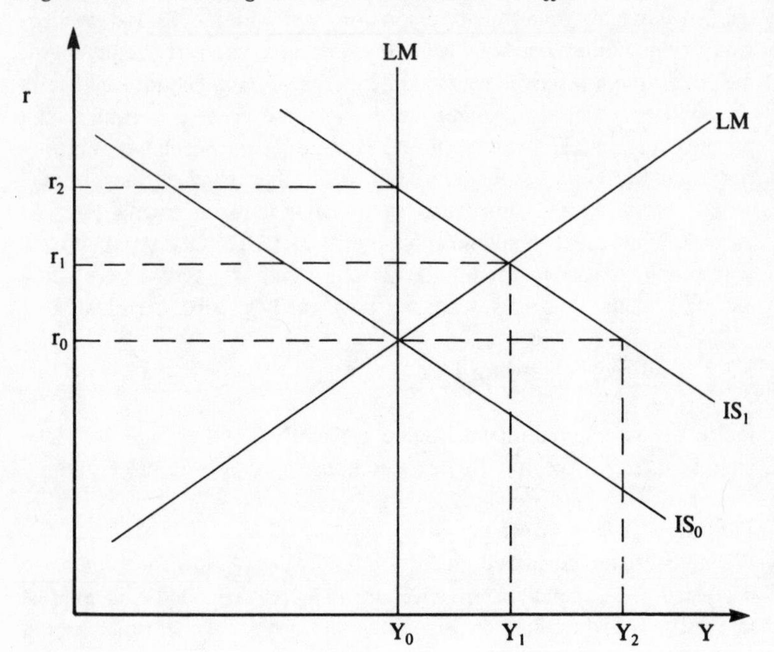

out in the long run. We now turn to consider how crowding out may arise due to the wealth effect following a bond-financed increase in government expenditure.

The wealth effect

Wealth exerts a positive influence on both consumption expenditure and the quantity of money demanded. Fiscal expansion financed by increased bond issues will lead to an increase in private sector wealth (owing to increased bond holdings) and therefore an increase in private consumption expenditure and the demand for money. Figure 5.5 illustrates how the wealth effect can be incorporated into the IS-LM model. The economy is initially in equilibrium at an income level of Y_0 i.e. the intersection of IS_0 and LM_0. A bond-financed fiscal expansion shifts the IS curve from IS_0 to IS_1 causing income to increase from Y_0 to Y_1 i.e. partial crowding out occurs due to the interest rate effect. The wealth effect on consumption will in turn reinforce the impact effect of fiscal expansion on aggregate demand, causing the IS curve to shift further outwards to the right as indicated by the arrows in Figure 5.5. The increase in private wealth will also increase the demand for money, causing the LM curve

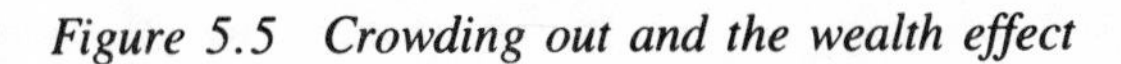

Figure 5.5 Crowding out and the wealth effect

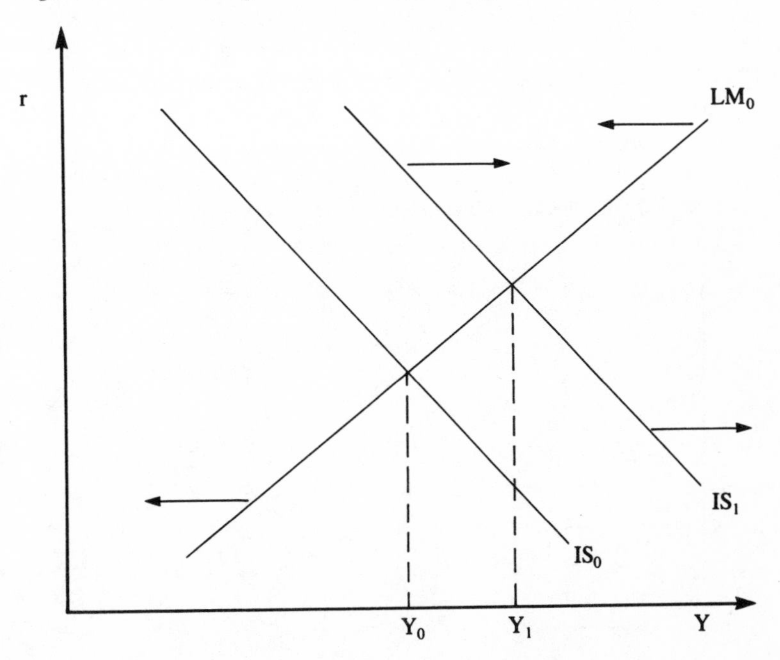

to shift upwards to the left, again indicated by the arrows in Figure 5.5. Whether income expands or contracts in the long run depends on the elasticity of consumption expenditure and that of money demand to changes in wealth, i.e. on the relative shifts of the two curves. Complete crowding out would entail income returning to its initial level of Y_0 in the long run.

The expectations effect

In addition to the interest rate and wealth effects, crowding out may also occur due to an expectations effect. An expansionary fiscal policy might affect expectations regarding the future. If the private sector's confidence in the economic future is adversely affected by a budget deficit this could result in a reduction in private sector investment and/or an increase in the demand for money. This is demonstrated in Figure 5.6. The economy is initially in equilibrium at an income level of Y_0 i.e. the intersection of IS_0 and LM_0. An increase in government expenditure shifts the IS curve to the right from IS_0 to IS_1 causing the equilibrium level of income to rise from Y_0 to Y_1. Any adverse effect on confidence will however cause the IS curve to shift inwards to the left and the LM curve upwards to the left, as indicated by the arrows in Figure 5.6. If crowding out is complete, income will return to Y_0.

Figure 5.6 Crowding out and the expectations effect

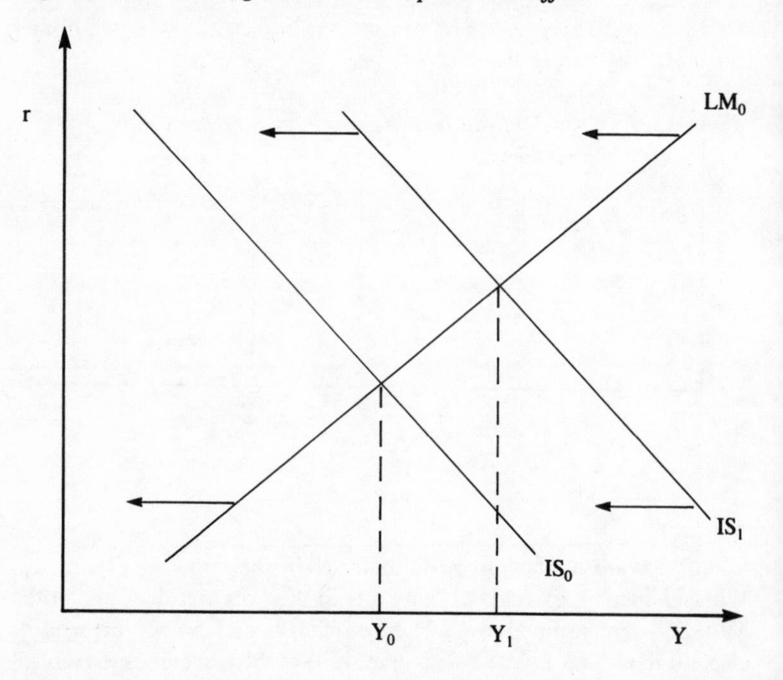

The price level effect

So far we have considered the three main reasons why indirect crowding out may occur at less than full employment. If, however, the economy is initially at full employment then an increase in government expenditure must in the long run result in the complete crowding out of private sector expenditure as income cannot rise above its full employment level. This is demonstrated in Figure 5.7. The economy is initially at full employment (Y_F) i.e. the intersection of IS_0 and LM_0. An increase in government expenditure will shift the IS curve to the right from IS_0 to IS_1 and generate a rise in the general price level. The rise in the price level will cause a decrease in the real value of the money supply (shifting the LM curve upwards to the left) and wealth fixed in nominal terms (shifting the IS curve inwards to the left). In the long run full employment equilibrium is re-established where the IS and LM curves intersect along the vertical line at Y_F. It is interesting to note that for complete crowding out to take place through this full employment price level effect, the long-run aggregate supply curve must be vertical. We will discuss this case more fully in section 5.5.

Figure 5.7 Crowding out and the price level effect at full employment

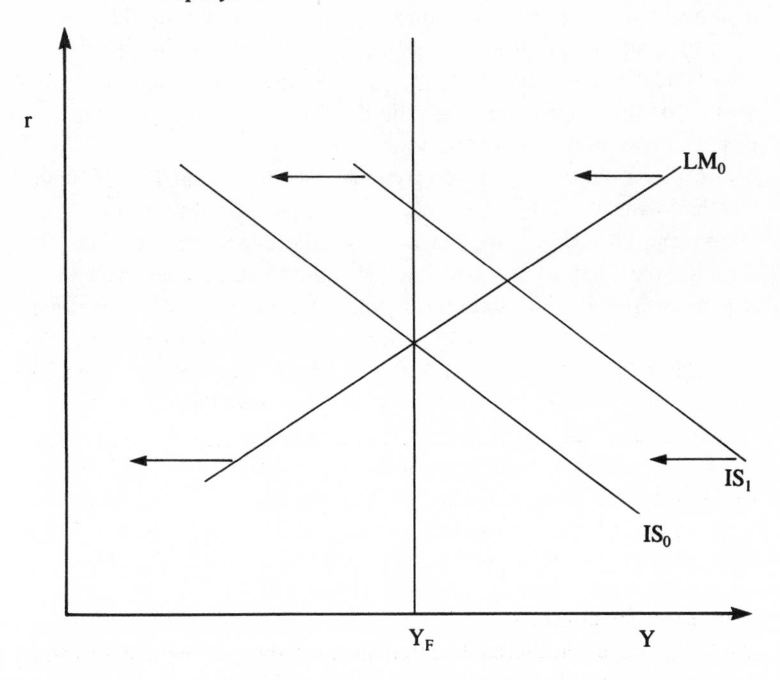

5.4 THE GOVERNMENT BUDGET CONSTRAINT AND THE CONTROVERSY OVER THE POWER OF FISCAL POLICY

Having discussed the Keynesian–monetarist debate on whether fiscal policy matters using the standard IS-LM model of a closed economy we now consider what effect the introduction of the government budget constraint into the analysis has on the predictions of the power of fiscal policy.

The effect of incorporating a government budget constraint into the standard IS-LM model was first examined by Ott and Ott (1965) and Christ (1968) but perhaps the main impetus to the discussion of this development came from Blinder and Solow (1973). The central proposition in this analysis is that long-run equilibrium in a macroeconomic model requires both stock and flow equilibrium. If we assume a self-contained economy that is not growing over time, long-run equilibrium is not possible if there is a budget deficit because in order to finance the deficit the authorities would have to issue either bonds or money in which case the supply of financial assets would change, disturbing stock equilibrium. Long-run equilibrium requires a balanced government budget. In what follows we examine the effect the introduction of this requirement into the IS-LM model has on the analysis of the impact of fiscal expansion.

Consider Figure 5.8. The top panel depicts the normal IS-LM model and the lower panel the government budget position determined by the relationship between government expenditure and tax revenue. To simplify the analysis government expenditure (G) is assumed to be independent of income (hence the horizontal line) while tax revenues (T) increase as income increases. The slope of the tax function represents the marginal rate of tax (t) and is assumed to be constant. In Figure 5.8 positive values occur on either side of the horizontal axis, i.e. positive rates of interest upwards and positive values of government expenditure and tax revenue downwards from 0.

We start from a position of long-run full stock equilibrium at an income level Y_0 (the intersection of IS_0 and LM_0) with a balanced government budget, i.e. $G_0 = T$ at income level Y_0. An increase in government expenditure shifts the IS curve outwards to the right from IS_0 to IS_1 and the government expenditure function downwards from G_0 to G_1. At an income level of Y_1 (the intersection of IS_1 and LM_0) there is a budget deficit equal to AB. The re-establishment of full stock equilibrium

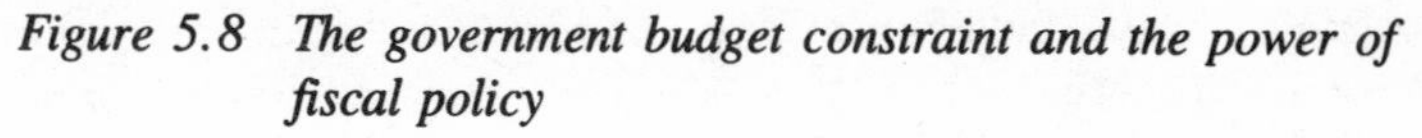

Figure 5.8 The government budget constraint and the power of fiscal policy

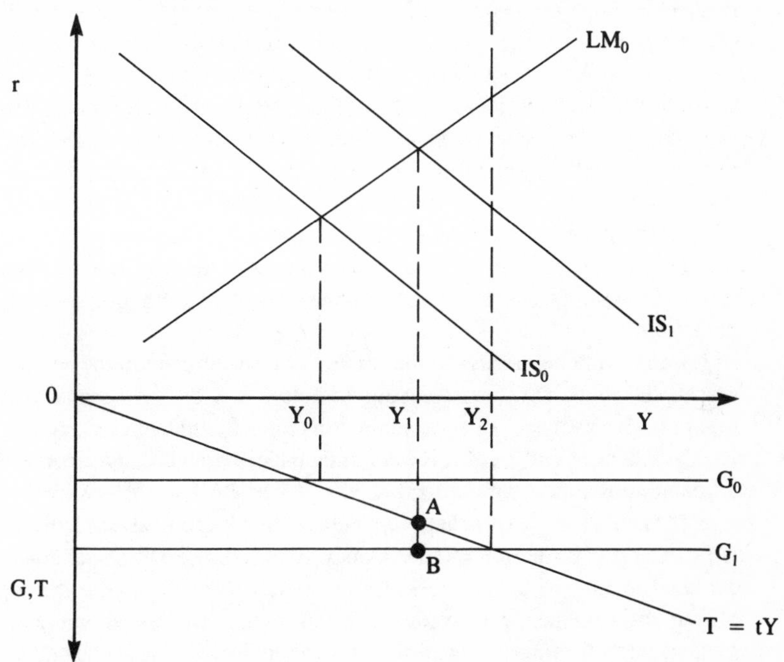

requires income rising to Y_2 such that government tax revenue equals the increased government expenditure thereby closing the budget deficit and restoring budgetary balance.

It is against this background that we now consider the impact of the wealth effects on consumption and the demand for money discussed earlier, in section 5.3.1. Where increased government expenditure is financed by bond sales private sector holdings of government bonds will increase as long as the budget deficit persists. If we assume that the wealth effect on consumption (which shifts the IS curve further outwards to the right) is stronger than that on the demand for money (which shifts the LM curve upwards to the left) the level of income rises and long-run equilibrium will be re-established when the budget is balanced at an income level of Y_2. In contrast if the wealth effect on the demand for money outweighs that on consumption then, although the immediate impact of increased government expenditure will be expansionary (i.e. income will initially rise from Y_0 to Y_1), in the long run the equilibrium level of income will continually decrease and the budget deficit will become larger, because as income falls tax revenues fall. In other words income will be continually driven further away from its long-run equilibrium level (Y_2) and there will be instability in the model. In summary, if the model is stable with the wealth-induced effects on consumption outweighing those on the demand for money then crowding out will be absent. On the other hand, if the wealth effect on the demand for money predominates the model is unstable and income will fall continually, i.e. complete crowding out in a stable model is not possible given the assumption of underemployment equilibrium and a constant price level.

Before turning to discuss the possibility of crowding out in the context of the AD-AS model it is interesting to note five additional points with regard to this analysis. First, assuming the model is stable, the long-run fiscal multiplier will be the same whether the increase in government expenditure is bond- or money-financed and will be equal to the reciprocal of the marginal tax rate. Where the increase in government expenditure is financed by an increase in the money supply the condition for long-run equilibrium will still necessitate income rising to Y_2 (see Figure 5.8). In this case there will be continual shifts of the LM curve downwards to the right as the money supply is increased until such time as the budget deficit is eliminated. Secondly, we have so far ignored the fact that a bond-financed increase in government expenditure involves increased interest payments on the outstanding stock of government bonds. In consequence, assuming the model is stable, a bond-financed increase in government expenditure will be more expansionary than a money-financed increase because increased interest payments from bond finance require a greater rise in real income to balance the government budget. In terms of Figure 5.8 the expenditure function will continue to shift downwards beyond G_1 until the budget is balanced. In the case of bond-financed fiscal expansion the final equilibrium level of income will then be to the right of Y_2. Thus we arrive at the paradoxical result that the long-run fiscal multiplier will be greater in the case where an increase in government expenditure is bond-financed rather than money-financed (this contrasts with the analysis discussed in section 5.2.2).

Thirdly, an objection to the predictions concerning the power of fiscal policy based on the inclusion of the government budget constraint in the model can be made on the grounds of rationality. The basis of this view is that the private sector will realize that increased bond issues will necessitate future increases in taxes to meet interest payments on and redemption of the bonds (see Barro 1974). These future tax liabilities will be discounted and their present value will be perceived to exactly offset the value of the bonds sold. In other words it would make no difference whether the government sold bonds or raised taxes to finance expenditure, as selling bonds will not affect the private sector's wealth. This means that there would be no wealth-induced shifts in the IS or LM curves and no need for the government budget to be balanced. The problem of instability would not arise. The impact of an increase in government expenditure would be the same whether financed by an increase in taxes or bond sales. Several arguments can be raised against this rationality view, or what has become known as the 'Ricardian equivalence theorem', including the argument that the private sector lacks the necessary degree of foresight and also that real income might rise, causing tax revenue to increase, thus obviating the need for future tax increases.

Fourthly, it is interesting to note that the extension of the model to the open economy renders the analysis much more complicated (see Chapter 2) and also makes the predictions ambiguous with regard to the long-run impact of fiscal policy on income and output. Suffice it to note that unlike the case of a closed economy long-run equilibrium does not require the government budget to be balanced. Finally an interesting point has been made by Sargent and Wallace (1985) regarding the distinction between bond and money financing of persistent public sector deficits. Tight monetary policy (i.e. bond finance) was traditionally regarded as not being inflationary. Sargent and Wallace question this view. Continuous increases in the outstanding stock of government bonds require continuous increases in the real rate of return on such debt. Eventually the required real rate of return exceeds the growth rate of the economy.

This presents the authorities with a problem. It is no longer possible to service the debt (repayment of principal plus interest rate payments) by issuing new public sector debt since the composition of private sector portfolios will be out of equilibrium. Hence either the debt must be (i) reduced by increased taxation or reduced government expenditure or (ii) serviced by monetary expansion. This implies that tight monetary policy now, without accommodating fiscal policy, will lead to increased inflation in the future. Alternatively slack monetary policy now, again without accommodating fiscal policy, will cause higher inflation now but lower future inflation as monetary policy is tightened. The critical implication of this analysis is that fiscal and monetary policy are interrelated and that therefore they must be co-ordinated. Note that in this analysis the assumption that inflation is a monetary phenomenon is maintained.

5.5 CROWDING OUT IN THE AD-AS MODEL

So far we have discussed the reasons why indirect crowding out may occur in terms of the IS-LM model of a closed economy. We now turn to consider crowding out in the context of the AD-AS model. This is demonstrated in Figure 5.9. You will recall from Chapter 1 that in monetarist and new classical analysis the long-run equilibrium (natural) levels of output (Y_N) and employment are determined by aggregate supply. Output and employment are fixed independently of the price level giving a vertical aggregate supply curve (AS) at Y_N where the price level is fully anticipated, i.e. the actual and expected price levels coincide.

Figure 5.9 Crowding out in the AD-AS model

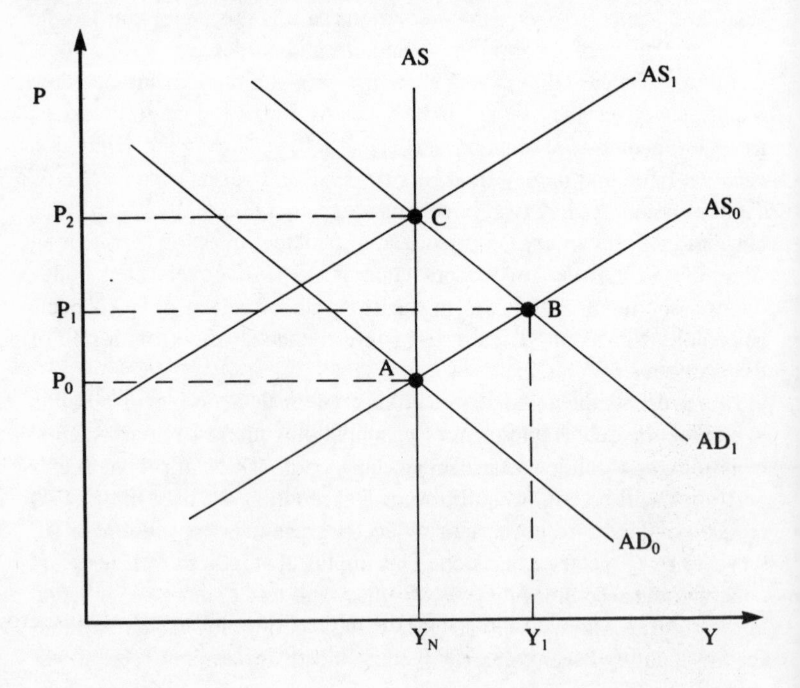

Aggregate demand shocks will only affect output and employment when they result in errors in price expectations, i.e. when the price level is not fully anticipated. In Figure 5.9 the positively sloped AS curves represent the response to aggregate demand shocks which result in output and employment deviating in the short run from their long-run equilibrium (natural) levels. As we will see, it is important to make a distinction between monetarist and new classical analysis in this respect.

Consider Figure 5.9. The economy is initially operating at P_0 Y_N (i.e. the triple intersection of AD_0 AS_0 and AS) at which point the price level is fully anticipated and output is at its long-run equilibrium level. Suppose the authorities increase their expenditure (to simplify the analysis we ignore the government budget constraint). The increase in government expenditure shifts the AD curve to the right from AD_0 to AD_1. In monetarist analysis this will result in the economy moving from point A to B in the short run, i.e. AD_1 intersects the positively sloped AS curve AS_0 at P_1 Y_1. The reason output and employment rise above their long-run equilibrium levels is because economic agents act on price expectations which are incorrect (expectations lag behind reality). Over time, as economic agents fully adjust their price expectations, the positively sloped AS curve will shift upwards from AS_0 to AS_1 and the economy will eventually move to point C, i.e. the triple intersection of AD_1 AS_1 and AS at P_2 Y_N. In other words in the long run the increase in government expenditure will result in the crowding out of an equal amount of private sector expenditure, i.e. crowding out will be complete. In contrast in new classical analysis, where price expectations are formed rationally, economic agents would revise their price expectations upwards immediately following an anticipated increase in government expenditure and the economy would move straight from A to C, i.e. complete crowding out will occur in the short run. Only where the increase in government expenditure is unanticipated will the economy go through the adjustment process discussed above (i.e. A to B to C) involving output increasing temporarily before returning to its long-run equilibrium level. In the long run crowding out will be complete.

5.6 CONCLUSION

In this chapter we have considered the issue of whether fiscal policy matters. Our discussion has largely focused on the Keynesian–monetarist debate within the context of the IS-LM model of a closed economy. From this discussion we can draw three main conclusions. First, the impact of fiscal expansion on aggregate demand will be determined not only by the relative slopes of the IS and LM curves but also by the way in which it is financed. Secondly, it is important to distinguish between the short- and long-run impact of fiscal expansion on income. Thirdly, once the government budget constraint is incorporated into the model, long-run equilibrium requires a balanced government budget with interesting consequences for the predictions of the long-run impact of fiscal expansion.

Finally brief mention needs to be made of the empirical evidence on the potency of fiscal policy to influence aggregate demand. Empirical evidence on crowding out has largely involved the use of large-scale econometric models to simulate the effects of policy changes under various assumptions. The problem with these simulations is that they reflect the properties of the respective models in question which in turn reflect the *a priori* beliefs of the model-builder. This means that simulation of macroeconomic models does not give a completely objective insight into the issue of the potency of fiscal policy. Given the ambiguous nature of the empirical evidence, the debate over the extent of crowding out is likely to continue and remain a controversial area.

6. Business Cycles

6.1 INTRODUCTION

In this chapter we examine the nature of the business cycle (section 6.2). This is followed by a discussion of the various theories which purport to explain the existence of the cycle. In section 6.3 we look at the early theories and discuss the equilibrium business cycle and political business cycle theories in sections 6.4 and 6.5 respectively. Our conclusions are presented in section 6.6.

At this early stage of the development of the analysis, it is worth noting that the methodology adopted in this chapter is different from that used in earlier chapters. In previous chapters comparative statics was used to demonstrate the various macroeconomic themes and, in that sense, the analysis was timeless. In this chapter we are concerned with the movement of output or real income over time so that the basis of the analysis is economic dynamics.

6.2 THE NATURE OF THE BUSINESS CYCLE

The business cycle (or trade cycle as it is sometimes called) can be defined as periodic fluctuations in the pattern of economic activity. This, of course, requires some precision about the meaning of economic activity. One measure often used is deviations of actual real GDP from its trend value. A simple stylized graphical representation of this definition is provided in Figure 6.1.

Within this framework a business cycle can be described by referring to:

i. the period of the cycle;
ii. the amplitude of the cycle;
iii. the degree of dampening experienced within the cycle.

The period of the cycle can be measured by the time gap between

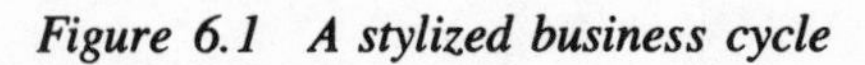

Figure 6.1 A stylized business cycle

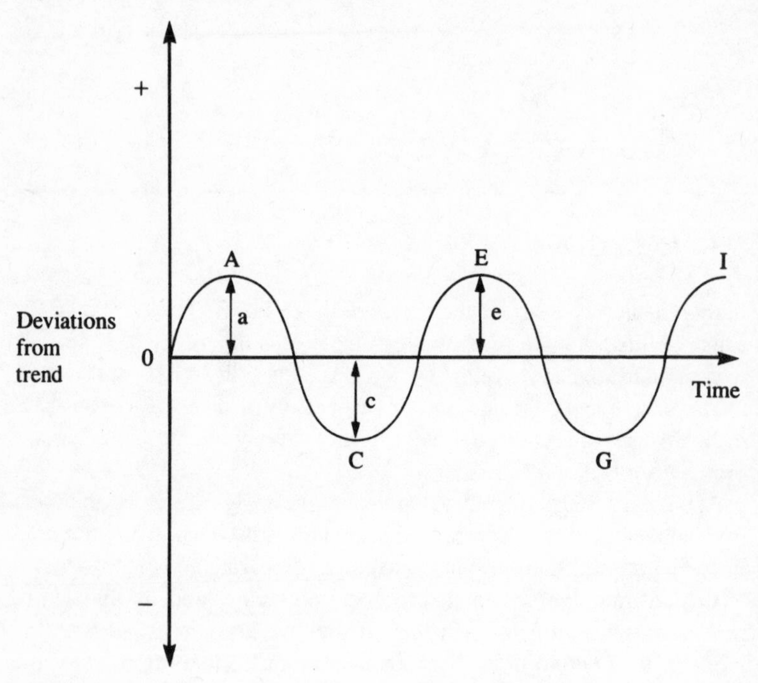

successive peaks, e.g. A to E or E to I. An alternative measure is the time gap between successive troughs such as C to G. The amplitude of the cycle gives an indication of its severity and may be measured by the gap between a peak and the succeeding trough a + c, or for that matter between a trough and the succeeding peak e.g. c + e. So it can be seen that these measures are not completely free from ambiguity except in the case where the fluctuations are perfectly regular from one period to another. Dampening refers to whether the cycle will decline in severity, or increase. Positive dampening is depicted in Figure 6.2a, where the amplitude of the cycles gradually decreases over time. Conversely Figure 6.2b shows the case of negative dampening, where the amplitude of the cycles increases over time. Finally, in this connection, it should be noted that Figure 6.1 shows a complete absence of dampening as the amplitude of the cycles remains constant.

Figure 6.1 can also be used to distinguish between different phases

Figure 6.2 Positive and negative dampening

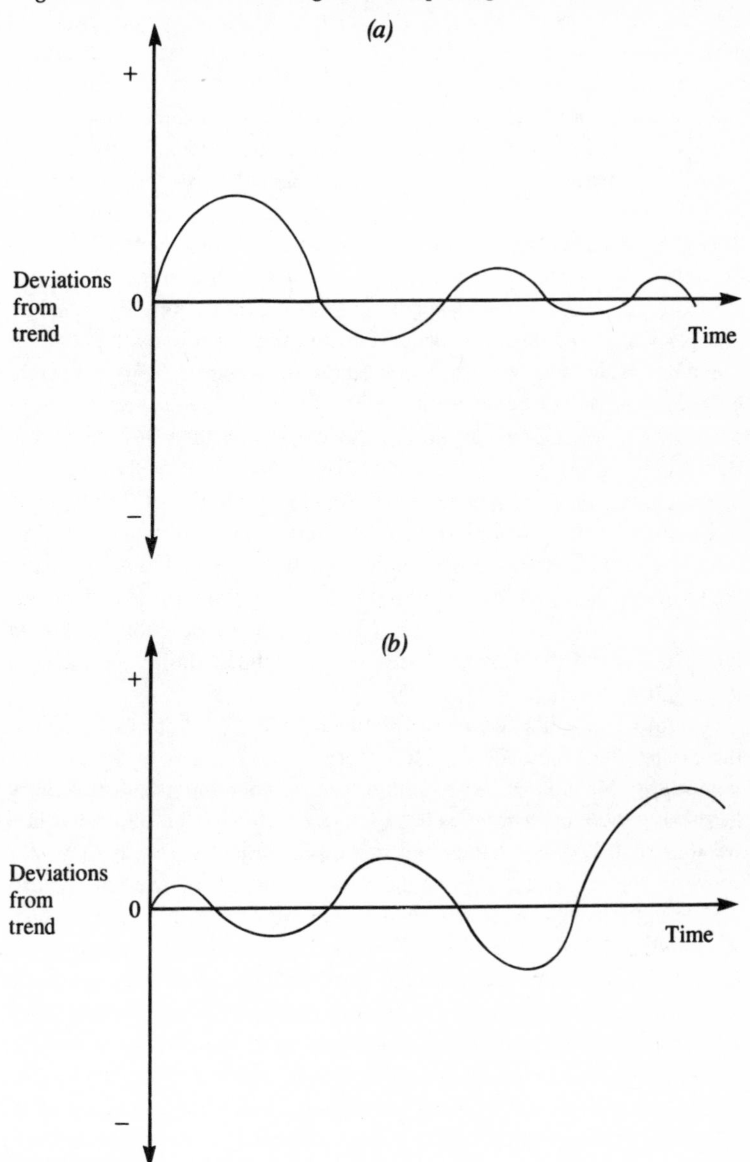

of the cycle. The movement from the peak (A) to the trough (C) is termed the contractionary phase and that from the trough (C) to the peak (E) the expansionary phase. Sometimes the peaks and troughs are also termed the 'upper' and 'lower' turning points respectively. Again the terms boom and depression are often used in connection with the business cycle. These terms refer to the period of rapid expansion and contraction respectively before the movement tends to flatten out near the top and the bottom of the cycle.

The very existence of the cycle has been questioned – see, for example, McCulloch (1975) – since, in practice, observed cycles are far less regular than that depicted in Figure 6.1. This permits the argument that the very irregularity of observed time series suggests the absence of regular cycles so that there is no need for an economic theory to explain the cycle. In contrast there exists a substantive body of literature produced by a variety of sources including the National Bureau of Economic Research (e.g. Mintz 1969) which is very supportive of the existence of cycles, but cycles which do not possess the regularity of that depicted in Figure 6.1. In a similar vein, controversy exists over the period of the cycle. Long swings in economic activity (i.e. over 50 to 60 years) are termed Kondratieff cycles. Other economists claim to have identified shorter periods such as 15 to 20 years, but the more common interpretation of the term cycle refers to the much shorter period of 3 to 5 years.

A number of other features of the cycle need to be discussed. First, the existence of the cycle is also observed in a number of series other than real GDP such as, for example, prices, unemployment, inventory holdings and interest rates. These series can further be described in a number of ways. First, they can move procyclically, that is they may move in the same direction as the cycle, such as, for example, prices which tend to rise with positive deviations of GDP from its trend. Alternatively, they can move in a contracyclical manner. Unemployment provides an example of a contracyclical variable, since unemployment falls with positive deviations of GDP from its trend value. A second categorization can be made with respect to the timing of the variable and the cycle as measured by deviations of real GDP from its trend. The actual series may lead, lag or be contemporaneous with the main series. For example, unemployment is a 'lazy' indicator of economic activity since changes in unemployment generally lag behind changes in real GDP. Finally, the term coherence describes the degree of conformity of the various individual series to the cycle in economic activity.

To sum up this section, the business cycle may be represented by periodic but irregular fluctuations in real GDP from its trend. This pattern of behaviour is also observed in a number of other series. Thus any explanation of the cycle must address these features.

6.3 EARLY THEORIES OF THE BUSINESS CYCLE

Early explanations of the business cycle can be divided into linear and non-linear theories. We describe below representations of these two types of theories, both of which depend on the interaction of the multiplier and the accelerator. Basically, according to the multiplier, an autonomous rise in investment produces a more than proportionate rise in income but this very rise in income/output induces a further increase in investment as new capital stock is required to produce the increased output. Since the cost of capital equipment is greater than the annual value of its output, the increase in investment is larger than the increase in income which brought it about. This latter phenomenon is called the accelerator. Consequently the rise in income due to the multiplier will be reinforced by a further increase in investment, which will in turn have a multiplier effect on income. Any expansionary shock will, therefore, produce a rapid increase in income. Similarly any contraction in income will produce a strong downward effect, so the expansionary and contractionary phases of the business cycle can be explained through the interaction of the multiplier and accelerator.

A number of versions of linear theories exist (see, for example, Samuelson 1939) but the simple model described below gives the general flavour of this type of model. Investment is assumed to depend on the lagged change in consumption:

$$I_t = v(C_t - C_{t-1}) \qquad (6.1)$$

where v is termed the accelerator coefficient.

Consumption is assumed to be proportional to lagged income:

$$C_t = bY_{t-1} \qquad (6.2)$$

where b is the marginal propensity to consume.

In this simple model equilibrium occurs where saving equals investment so that:

$$Y_t - bY_{t-1} = I_t \tag{6.3}$$

Substituting (6.1) and (6.2) into (6.3) and rearranging produces the second-order difference equation in income:

$$Y_t = b(1 + v)Y_{t-1} - (vb)Y_{t-2} \tag{6.4}$$

or more generally:

$$Y_t = \alpha\, Y_{t-1} - \beta\, Y_{t-2} \tag{6.4a}$$

where $\alpha = b(1 + v)$ and $\beta = vb$

Since income in the current period depends positively on income in the previous period and negatively on income two periods previously it is intuitively plausible that periodic fluctuations in income are possible given appropriate values for v and b. In fact a wide range of patterns of behaviour are possible including regular, damped and explosive fluctuations depending on the values of the two coefficients α and β. For a more precise discussion of the possible outcomes, the interested reader is referred to the more formal discussion of solutions to difference equations contained in texts on mathematical economics.

The problem with the linear difference equation representation of the business cycle is that the values of the coefficients necessary to produce cycles appear almost by chance. In contrast, non-linear theories in the tradition of Hicks (1950) offer sound economic reasons for expansion and contraction and also the turning points. Hicks's development of the business cycle depends on the operation of floors and ceilings to the path of growth of real income. The basic idea is that the interaction of the multiplier and accelerator produces growth in real output which is not sustainable in the long run because full employment acts as a brake to further growth. The slowdown in output reduces investment through the operation of the accelerator so that real output falls, reinforcing the reduction in induced investment. Eventually the level of income falls to that level compatible with 'long-run' investment so that income starts to grow again. This, in turn, induces more investment through the accelerator so that the expansionary process commences again. The repetition of this behaviour provides the explanation for the existence of the business cycle.

The model is developed more formally in Figure 6.3. The vertical axis refers to the logarithm of real output and the horizontal axis time. The

Figure 6.3 The Hicks business cycle

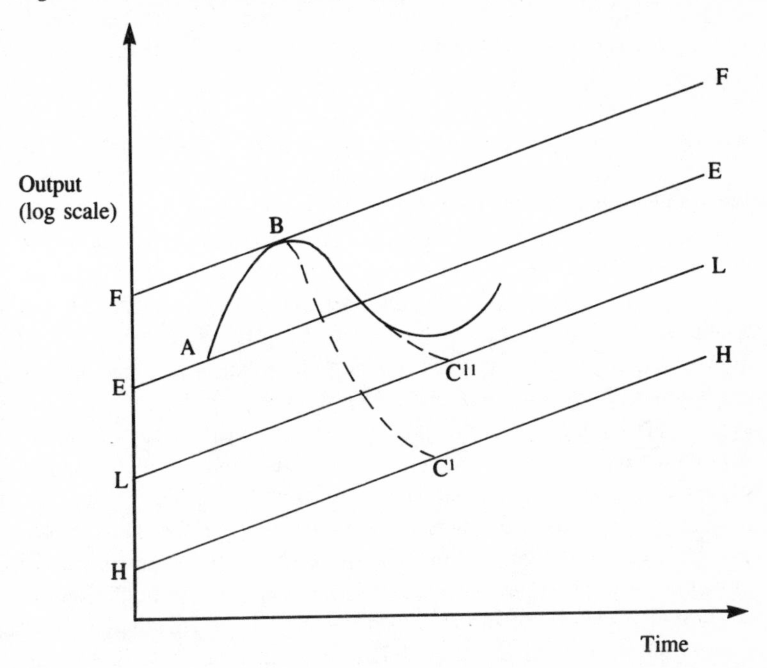

line HH refers to 'long-run' investment with a steady growth in investment being implied by the upward-sloping straight line. The line FF represents the full employment growth path of real income. EE and LL are upper and lower equilibrium lines for the growth of real income. Their slopes are determined by long-term investment, i.e. the slope of HH. EE is an equilibrium or natural rate of growth in the sense that the economy could progress along this line given the level of long-term investment plus the value of investment induced through the accelerator. The model is, however, similar to the Harrod growth model since it is 'razor-edged' inasmuch as any disturbance will cause the growth of actual income to depart from the equilibrium path.

Assume, for example, that we start from point A on EE and that there is a random expansionary disturbance. Income will grow more rapidly than that described by EE and will eventually hit a ceiling given by the growth of full employment output on FF, say at point B. At this point the rate of increase of growth of real output is reduced to that given by the ceiling FF so that induced investment falls to that level consistent with the natural rate of growth, i.e. that rate of growth of real income depicted by EE. The reduction in investment causes the rate of growth in real income to fall along the line BC^{I} towards EE. However, as income falls its rate of growth is less than that given by the natural rate so that induced investment declines further and income falls below EE. But Hicks argues that the path BC^{I} is too pessimistic since it is unlikely that induced investment will become negative for any significant period of time. If induced investment is zero, then the only investment carried out will be that defined by the line HH. This will have the familiar multiplier effect on income which reduces the rate of decline of real output to, say, BC^{II} where intersection occurs with the line LL. Since the line LL is upward sloping the actual lower turning point will precede C^{II} as induced investment becomes positive, and the expansionary phase will recommence and the whole process repeats itself again. Note that in this explanation the coefficients are not constrained to specific values for cycles to be produced. All that is necessary is: (i) the relationship between consumption and income, (ii) the relationship between the rate of change of income and investment (the accelerator), (iii) the multiplier effect of changes in investment on income, and (iv) a limit to the growth of capacity output due to limited resources. These are not particularly onerous requirements.

The shocks, or 'chance divergences' as Hicks terms them, are essentially real shocks and there appears to be no explicit role for monetary changes. An opposing view is taken by monetarists, who argue that changes in the rate of monetary expansion are the dominant force behind the business cycle. Friedman and Schwartz (1963) argue that the evidence gleaned from US history shows that:

1. there is a one-to-one relationship between changes in money and those in prices and money income;
2. changes in the money stock cannot consistently be explained adequately by contemporaneous changes in money income and prices but rather are attributable to specific historical circumstances.

According to their arguments, it follows that money causes the changes in money income and prices. The transmission mechanism envisaged by Friedman and Schwartz follows the standard monetarist view. For pedagogic purposes, the assumed starting point is one where real per capita income, the stock of money and prices are all changing at a constant rate. Purely for illustrative purposes, the further simplification of constant real interest rates is introduced so that the key relationship is that between real income and money. A positive monetary shock induced by, say, open market operations will cause the banks' holdings of high-powered money to increase. In turn the banks will expand their assets in the form of purchase of additional securities and new loans in order to restore the desired relationship between holdings of high-powered money and other more profitable assets. In the wider context of the non-bank private sector a general adjustment of portfolios will take place, including substitution of additional money balances for both financial and real assets. This causes money income to rise. Eventually a new equilibrium will be established in which the growth paths of the variables are again constant and consistent with each other.

Friedman and Schwartz argue that the transition path to this new equilibrium will not be smooth, but will overshoot. One reason for this overshooting is that the rise in prices will be underestimated so that the quantity of excess real balances will be overestimated. This leads to an excessive rise in expenditure so that prices overshoot the new equilibrium path. A similar analysis arises from the concept of the augmented Phillips curve discussed in Chapter 3, section 3.3. Workers are fooled by a rise in money wages and believe that real wages have risen so that more labour is supplied and real output rises. However, as expectations catch up with price rises, employment and real output will start to fall and unemployment will finally return to the natural rate. Hence business cycles can be observed.

Monetarists believe empirical evidence shows that the dominant shocks to the economy have been caused by changes in the money supply for reasons unconnected with the demand for money. Hence it is appropriate to discuss the 'monetary' business cycle. In this stylized approach, expectations were assumed to be formed in the light of past experience of the behaviour of the variable concerned. Because of the time required for expectations to catch up with actual events, it was possible for economic agents to be fooled into believing that monetary changes were real changes – in the preceding analysis changes in money wages and nominal balances were confused with changes in the corresponding real variables. Eventually expectations caught up with actual changes so that the cycle could be termed a disequilibrium phenomenon. This contrasts with the business cycle theory developed by Lucas, which is examined in the following section.

6.4 THE EQUILIBRIUM BUSINESS CYCLE

The development of the theory of the equilibrium business cycle is presented in Lucas (1975) and (1977). The interested reader will find the 1977 paper more accessible.

The underlying rationale of the equilibrium business cycle follows the views of new classical economics summarized in Chapter 1, sections 1.2.3 and 1.3.3. It is based on the existence of a competitive equilibrium but one in which agents may misinterpret information so as to produce incorrect responses to price changes. In this sense it is similar to the monetarist explanation of the business cycle in which agents confuse monetary with real changes. It is also similar in another respect, since the shocks are essentially monetary shocks. A major difference occurs between the two approaches since expectations in the equilibrium business cycle approach are assumed to be formed according to the 'rational' expectations hypothesis rather than with reference to past events as in the orthodox monetarist approach (discussed more fully in the appendix to Chapter 3).

The three key props to the theory of the equilibrium business cycle are:

1. the Lucas supply hypothesis, or the 'surprise' supply curve as it is sometimes called;
2. the structure of information available to economic agents;
3. incorporation of an accelerator mechanism into the analysis.

Following the analysis presented in Chapter 1, the Lucas supply hypothesis – see, for example, Lucas (1973) – may be written as:

$$y_t = y^n_t + \beta(p_t - E_{t-1}\, p_t) + \epsilon_t \qquad (6.5)$$

where y, y^n and p are the natural logarithms of actual output, normal output and prices respectively. E refers to the expected value with expectations formed rationally given the information set available in period $t-1$. ϵ is a random error term and normal output is defined as that level of output where the expected price level equals the actual price level and is, therefore, analogous to the natural rate of unemployment.

Note this supply function is written in terms of output rather than inputs as is more usually the case as, for example, in Phillips curve analysis. The term surprise function is derived from the fact that output responds positively to the gap between actual and expected price levels. This leads to the second underlying principle, the structure of the information set available to the economic agents. Producers are faced by what is known as the 'signal extraction problem', that is they receive a signal which contains information concerning changes in both absolute and relative prices. The problem for the producer is to extract from this signal information upon which to make the correct response, that is to distinguish between relative and absolute price changes.

More precisely, agents are viewed as operating within markets which are 'islands'. These islands are subject to: (i) real shocks which are local or peculiar to the islands in which the agent operates and (ii) monetary shocks which affect the so-called island markets in general. The information set available to the agents contains the market clearing price for the island in which he operates but not those for the other markets. It should be noted that the producer can only move between islands at the end of periods and even then capital stocks remain in place. These assumptions explain why the term 'islands' is used.

The problem for the producer is to try to distinguish between changes in relative prices and absolute price changes. A supply response is necessary for the former but not for the latter. The producers are rational and use past information concerning real and nominal shocks to form an expectation of the current market clearing price in the island in which they operate. Their response follows the surprise supply function depicted in equation (6.5) so that if the price is higher than expected a positive supply response is in order and producers expand output. Lucas argues that the response must be quick since, in the competitive environment of the hypothesis, failure to increase output will result in loss of business to the other producers.

The analysis carried out so far fails to explain the persistence of departures of actual income from its normal level which is one of the main characteristics of the business cycle. This can easily be seen by defining cyclical output (y^c) as:

$$y^c_t = y_t - y^n_t \tag{6.6}$$

Substituting for $y_t - y^n_t$ from (6.6) in (6.5) gives:

$$y^c_t = \beta(p_t - E_{t-1}\, p_t) + \epsilon_t \tag{6.7}$$

The terms on the right-hand side (6.7) are both random processes since the term in brackets represents a forecast error which is random according to the rational expectations hypothesis and the term ϵ is random by definition. These terms do not, therefore, offer any explanation of the persistent movements observed in the business cycle. This was achieved by the inclusion of output lagged one period in the supply equation. The rationale for this was based on an accelerator-type mechanism, i.e. the third of the underlying principles noted above. The required increase in supply following an unexpected rise in prices could only be achieved if spare capacity existed. In the case of the absence of spare capacity, investment is needed to produce the extra capacity with which to meet the perceived increased demand for output. Inclusion of this accelerator-type mechanism explained the existence of persistence even given the assumptions of (i) market clearing (ii) the natural rate hypothesis and (iii) the rational expectations hypothesis.

The information structure assumed in the development of the equilibrium business cycle is subject to potential criticism. If agents are confused and find it difficult to distinguish between local (i.e. appropriate to their island market) and aggregate shocks, why don't they sample the other markets to obtain relevant information? Sampling involves additional cost but the benefits derived in the form of extra information obtained from the signals could easily exceed the losses due to the additional cost. Presumably in practice as distinct from the more rarified environment of the Walrasian auctioneer, agents are already collecting and processing information such as production costs and market statistics up to the point where the marginal benefit equals the marginal cost. This has the implication that the costs of obtaining additional information regarding the other markets is excessive. A second criticism concerns the lack of explicit interdependence of the various markets. Much of economic theorizing within the Keynesian and monetarist traditions emphasizes the interdependence of the various markets, which helps to explain the co-movement of the various economic variables within a trade cycle.

The theory developed by Lucas envisages business cycles as primarily caused by monetary shocks. Kydland and Prescott in a series of articles (see, e.g., 1980) used a similar framework to demonstrate that an equilibrium business cycle could be generated by technological and fiscal changes. This last point emphasizes that the equilibrium business cycle theory is neutral with respect to causation of the cycle and throws no light on whether monetary or real shocks are the dominant cause of cycles. One of the assumptions underlying equilibrium business cycle theory is the rationality of the relevant economic agents. In the next section we move on to consider an alternative theory which moves to the opposite end of the spectrum and assumes that economic agents are myopic.

6.5 THE POLITICAL BUSINESS CYCLE

The rationale underlying this approach is quite simple. Voters are fooled by democratic governments. As an election approaches, governments will pursue expansionary policies in order to win votes. After the election it is often necessary to adopt corrective (i.e. contractionary) policies so as to dampen down inflationary tendencies. These changes in macroeconomic policy produce the cyclical path observed in the business cycle. A more formal explanation now follows.

This approach is based on the belief that political parties have the primary goal of winning the next election. Associated with this objective is the assumption that economic factors have a strong influence on the choice made by the voters, so it is sensible for governments to bear this in mind when designing economic policies. In terms of economic jargon there is a 'reaction function' linking government policy to the state of the economy. In particular the two primary influences are: (i) the level of unemployment and (ii) the rate of inflation. The government is assumed to maximize an objective function dependent on the minimization of these two variables. It is further assumed that the government's achievement of these two objectives is constrained by an augmented Phillips curve (see Chapter 3, section 3.3) so that it is not possible to reduce both variables simultaneously. The government has, therefore, to choose a 'trade-off' between these two variables and the choice made as to the trade-off will vary at different times. In particular as the date of the election approaches, falls in the level of unemployment will become more important than inflation, so there is a tendency to follow expansionary policies prior to the election date. Conversely, after the election there is a strong incentive for the government to pursue anti-inflationary policies which tend to raise the level of unemployment. The mathematical solution to this maximization problem is beyond the scope of this text, but it is sufficient to note that the path of unemployment implied by the solution takes the general form shown in Figure 6.4 where A, B and C are the election dates.

It is interesting to consider the rationale underlying the behaviour of the voters in this scenario. First, they are assumed to form expectations adaptively which means that more recent events are more important in

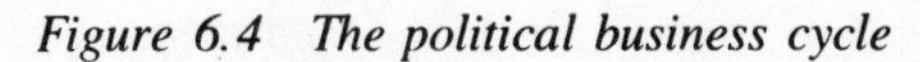

Figure 6.4 The political business cycle

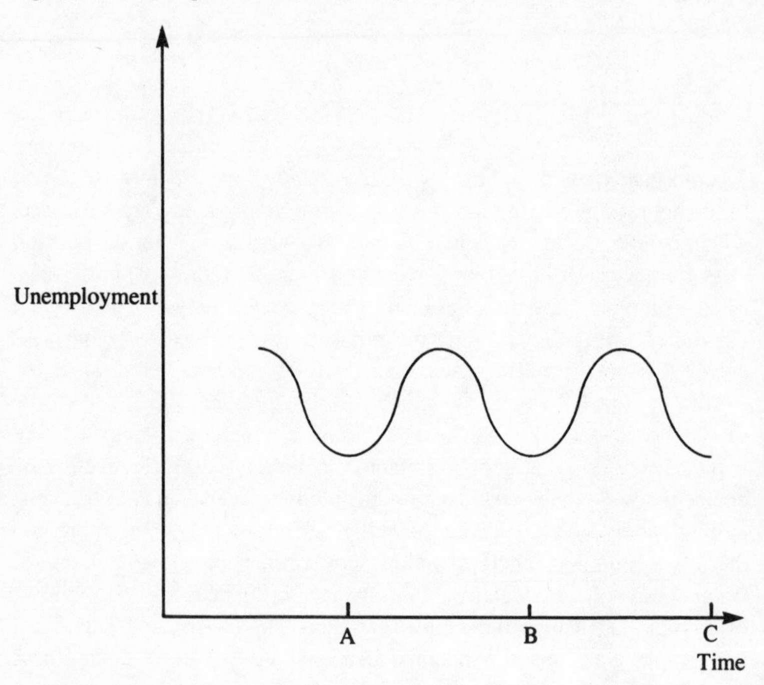

their voting decisions. This accounts for the incentive for governments to pursue anti-inflationary policies immediately after an election so that the memory of the rise in unemployment, necessary to cure inflation given the existence of the Phillips curve, will have decayed by the time of the next election. Secondly, agents are myopic in the sense that they do not look into the future. Myopia also arises because the voters are continually fooled by the government's 'stop–go' conduct of macroeconomic policy.

At this stage it is worthwhile recapitulating the economic theory underlying the political business cycle. First, expectations are assumed to be formed according to the adaptive expectations hypothesis. This is a dubious assumption given the well-known defects of this approach – in particular ignoring any other information apart from past values of the variable concerned. Secondly, it is assumed that the government can manipulate economic variables. This assumption requires the absence of: (i) complete crowding out in the case of fiscal policy, and (ii) short-run neutrality of money in the case of monetary policy. Clearly this view of the business cycle is incompatible with the new classical view. Thirdly, in line with our comments regarding the formation of expectations, there is the implied assumption that the voters do not learn from the past experience of the electoral cycle and are unable to see through the government's policy.

The theory can also be criticized from the political aspect. First there is the implied adoption of the 'median voter theory', whereby the parties' policies are designed to capture the votes of the centre. This implies that both parties will offer similar policies to attract the centre and ignores the fact that the parties are likely to have ideological aims in addition to that of obtaining power. Secondly, the theory seems to be more appropriate for countries with fixed election dates, such as the US, rather than countries such as the UK where election dates are variable. In this latter type of political system it is more likely that the date of the election becomes endogenous so as to fit the timing of the cycle rather than vice versa.

6.6 CONCLUSION

We have surveyed a number of theories of the business cycle. At the start of this chapter we introduced the idea that there is some dispute as to whether such a cycle exists. Our broad conclusion is that the evidence does support the existence of business cycles but that they are far less regular in period and amplitude than those described by purely mathematical methods. A number of theories explaining the existence of the cycle exist and there is certainly no unanimity on which theory is most appropriate. In many ways the debate follows that discussed in Chapter 1. Hence the theory of Hicks follows the Keynesian approach, suggesting that real factors cause the cycle. Monetarist theory follows the standard monetarist approach with the dominant influence being ascribed to monetary impulses but with a slow response to the changes. This approach is fairly easily reconciled with the Hicksian view of the cycle by the incorporation in that theory of the view that monetary shocks are the dominant factor in the creation of cycles together with an acceptance of a long-run vertical Phillips curve.

The equilibrium business cycle theory is quite distinct from the earlier theories and reflects the new classical stance with its adoption of market clearing and rational expectations. Within this framework, the business cycle arises from the errors made by agents because of the signal extraction problem. Persistence is explained by an accelerator-type mechanism. As we have discussed earlier, it seems reasonable to criticize the information structure assumed in this approach. Finally the political business cycle ascribes the existence of a cycle to government macroeconomic policy.

7. Conclusion

From the discussion of the preceding chapters, it is apparent that a considerable degree of controversy exists with regard to the different schools' perceptions both of the nature of the economy and also of how it operates. This controversy naturally spills over into differing views of the role of government macroeconomic policy. In this last chapter we briefly summarize these views, relating our comments to the discussions contained in the earlier chapters.

During the 1950s and 1960s the prevailing orthodoxy in macroeconomic theory and policy was that of Keynesian economics. Central to Keynesian economics is the belief that capitalist economies are inherently unstable – see for example the Keynesian view of the trade cycle in Chapter 6, section 6.3. This results in the belief that, after an economic shock, it will take a long time for full employment equilibrium to be reattained in the absence of corrective government policy. Keynesians therefore stress the need for active interventionist policies and, in particular, hold the belief that demand management policies are essential to achieve full employment. In the 1950s and 1960s primary importance was attached to fiscal policy (see Chapter 5, section 5.2) with only a minor role being envisaged for monetary policy, and even then it was perceived as a back-up to fiscal policy. As discussed in Chapter 1, section 1.3.1, this implies a relatively steep IS curve and a relatively flat LM curve with no real discussion of aggregate supply so that the IS-LM framework provided an adequate model for discussion of macroeconomic problems. The low importance attached to the role of money was probably more pronounced in the UK than elsewhere – see for example the Radcliffe Report (1959) which tended to remove any real role for money – and there was a tendency to regard the economy as if it was always in the liquidity trap.

From the late 1960s and early 1970s, the Keynesian orthodoxy increasingly came under attack as many economies began to experience both high unemployment and inflation (so-called stagflation). The theoretical attack came in the form of the 'monetarist' counter-revolution with particular emphasis on the belief that (i) the demand for money was stable (see Chapter 4, section 4.4.4) so that money was an important determinant of the level of economic activity (see Chapter 4 in general), and (ii) the Phillips curve was vertical in the long run (see Chapter 3, in particular section 3.3). As far as the economy is concerned, monetarists argue that western economies are inherently stable around the natural rate of unemployment unless disturbed by erratic government macro-economic policy. After such a disturbance, monetarists believe, the economy will return fairly rapidly to the neighbourhood of the long-run equilibrium in the vicinity of the natural rate of unemployment (see Chapter 3 section 3.3 again for a discussion of this point). Because of their belief in the inherent self-regulating properties of the economy, monetarists question the need for discretionary demand management policies. In fact they often argue that, given the current state of knowledge, attempts to fine-tune the economy can increase instability. In terms of the discussion contained within Chapter 6, section 6.2, this is the same as arguing that the amplitude of the business cycle will be enhanced rather than reduced by government policy.

This debate over the role and conduct of stabilization policy was neatly summarized by Modigliani (1977) in his presidential address to the American Economic Association:

> the distinguishing feature of the monetarist school and the real issues of disagreement with nonmonetarists is not monetarism, but rather the role that should probably be assigned to stabilization policies. Nonmonetarists accept what I regard to be the fundamental practical message of *The General Theory*: that a private enterprise economy using an intangible money *needs* to be stabilized, *can* be stabilized, and therefore *should* be stabilized by appropriate monetary and fiscal policies. Monetarists by contrast take the view that there is no serious need to stabilize the economy; that even if there were a need, it could not be done, for stabilization policies would be more likely to increase than to decrease instability.

The interesting point about the so-called monetarist counter-revolution is that it is fairly easy to encompass its main features within the previous Keynesian paradigm. It is only necessary to incorporate (i) a stable demand for money with a relatively low interest elasticity and (ii) the natural rate of unemployment, to achieve monetarist predictions. Of course this oversimplifies the differences between the two schools. In fact, as we have already discussed, monetarists in contrast to Keynesians believe in the inherent stability and fairly quick adjustment of the economy in response to disturbances. They also tend to have a healthy respect for free markets and an inherent distrust of government behaviour.

More recently, developments in macroeconomics associated with new classical economics have further called into question the role of stabilization policies. As we saw in Chapter 1, section 1.3, the key theoretical difference between the new classical and both the Keynesian and monetarist schools is the assumption/belief that markets continually clear. In association with the belief in rational expectations (see the appendix to Chapter 3) this produces the view that the economy will adjust almost immediately to perceived changes in policy or shocks, through price changes. It is only unanticipated policy changes or shocks that will produce real effects such as changes in employment and output. Consequently demand management policies are completely ineffective in influencing real as distinct from nominal variables. In a similar vein the costs of reducing inflation are held to be minimal provided the policy adopted is credible. In Chapter 6, section 6.4, we showed how the assumptions concerning the information structure available to agents could produce an equilibrium business cycle. Our own summing up suggested that these informational assumptions were not fully credible. It is also interesting to conjecture that, although often termed monetarism version 2, the new classical school has little in common with orthodox or traditional monetarism with the latter's belief in slower adjustment (although the adjustment in orthodox monetarism is quicker than that envisaged in Keynesian economics). In fact it may be argued that orthodox monetarism has more in common with Keynesian economics than the new classical school.

Against this background increasing attention has been given to the supply side of the economy and the attempt to influence output and employment by *microeconomic* policies directed towards increasing aggregate supply by altering the response of individuals and firms to changing conditions and market demands. Indeed over recent years many western governments have largely eschewed aggregate demand management policies and have instead turned to supply-side policies to improve the performance of their economies. In the UK, for example, the Conservative government in office since 1979 has given a primary role to supply-side policies and has concentrated its policy to improve the supply side of economy in three main directions: (i) cutting marginal income tax rates to increase the incentive to work; (ii) trade union reform to promote greater flexibility of wages and working practices; and (iii) privatization to make the market for goods and services (and capital) function more efficiently. While a discussion of the theoretical arguments underlying and empirical evidence on these and other supply-side policies is beyond the scope of this text, the reader should be aware that the nature and effectiveness of supply-side policies has itself been the subject of considerable controversy.

In the last ten years or so there have been many important developments in macroeconomic theory. Probably the most important is that of incorporating the rational expectations hypothesis into standard macroeconomic models. A second development is the use of more general portfolio models to explain, to take just two examples, the demand for money (see Chapter 4, sections 4.4.3 and 4.5.1) and the determination of exchange rates (see Chapter 2, section 2.6.2). These developments modify to some extent the policy implications of more restricted models and are likely to continue. Our summary also tends to indicate that certain key international aspects of macroeconomics discussed in Chapter 2 still remain to be fully incorporated into mainstream theory. A tendency still exists for international aspects to be included in some texts as a sort of appendage or concluding chapter rather than being fully integrated into the main body of thought. To take just one example, the demand for money is often discussed in terms of domestic factors excluding foreign rates of interest from the determinants. Similarly the Phillips curve is generally discussed within the environment of expectations being formed about future inflation without reference to foreign price changes. It is likely that future developments will pay greater attention to the international aspects of both macroeconomic theory and policy.

Bibliography

Alt, J.E. and Chrystal, K.A. (1983), *Political Economics*, Brighton: Wheatsheaf Books.

Attfield, C.L.F., Demery, D. and Duck, N.W. (1985), *Rational Expectations in Macroeconomics: An Introduction to Theory and Evidence*, Oxford: Basil Blackwell.

Barro, R.J. (1974), 'Are Government Bonds Net Wealth?', *Journal of Political Economy*, November/December.

Barro, R.J. (1976), 'Rational Expectations and the Role of Monetary Policy', *Journal of Monetary Economics*, January.

Barro, R.J. (1977), 'Long Term Contracting, Sticky Prices and Monetary Policy', *Journal of Monetary Economics*, July.

Barro, R.J. and Fischer, S. (1976), 'Recent Developments in Monetary Theory', *Journal of Monetary Economics*, April.

Baumol, W.J. (1952), 'The Transactions Demand for Cash: An Inventory Theoretic Approach', *Quarterly Journal of Economics*, November.

Begg, D.K.H. (1982), *The Rational Expectations Revolution in Macroeconomics: Theories and Evidence*, Oxford: Philip Allan.

Blinder, A.S. and Solow, R.M. (1973), 'Does Fiscal Policy Matter?', *Journal of Public Economics*, November.

Blinder, A.S. and Solow, R.M. (1976), 'Does Fiscal Policy Still Matter?', *Journal of Monetary Economics*, November.

Branson, W.H. and Buiter, W.H. (1983), 'Monetary and Fiscal Policy with Flexible Exchange Rates', in J.S. Bhandari and B.H. Putnam (eds), *Economic Interdependence and Flexible Exchange Rates*, Cambridge, Mass: MIT Press.

Brunner, K. and Meltzer, A.H. (1968), 'Liquidity Traps for Money, Bank Credit and Interest Rates', *Journal of Political Economy*, February.

Buiter, W.H. (1980), 'The Macroeconomics of Dr. Pangloss: A Critical Survey of the New Classical Macroeconomics', *Economic Journal*, March.

Cagan, P. (1956), 'The Monetary Dynamics of Hyperinflation', in M. Friedman (ed.), *Studies in the Quantity Theory of Money*, Chicago: University of Chicago Press.

Carlson, K.M. and Spencer, R.W. (1975), 'Crowding Out and Its Critics', *Federal Reserve Bank of St Louis Monthly Review*, December.

Carter, M. and Maddock, R. (1984), *Rational Expectations: Macroeconomics for the 1980s?*, London: Macmillan.

Christ, C.F. (1968), 'A Simple Macroeconomic Model with a Government Budget Restraint', *Journal of Political Economy*, January/February.

Chrystal, K.A. (1983), *Controversies in Macroeconomics*, 2nd edition, Oxford: Philip Allan.

Chrystal, K.A. (1989), 'Overshooting Models of the Exchange Rate', in D. Greenaway (ed.), *Current Issues in Macroeconomics*, London: Macmillan.

Copeland, L. (1989), *Exchange Rates and International Finance*, Reading, Mass: Addison-Wesley.

Cross, R.B. (1982), *Economic Theory and Policy in the U.K.*, Oxford: Martin Robertson.

Dornbusch, R. (1976), 'Expectations and Exchange Rate Dynamics', *Journal of Political Economy*, December.

Fair, R.C. (1979), 'An Analysis of the Accuracy of Four Macro-econometric Models', *Journal of Political Economy*, August.

Fischer, S. (1977), 'Long-Term Contracts, Rational Expectations and the Optimal Money Supply Rule', *Journal of Political Economy*, February.

Fischer, S. (ed.) (1980), *Rational Expectations and Economic Policy*, Chicago: University of Chicago Press.

Fleming, J.M. (1962), 'Domestic Financial Policies under Fixed and Floating Exchange Rates', *IMF Staff Papers*, 9.

Frenkel, J.A. and Johnson, H.G. (eds) (1976), *The Monetary Approach to the Balance of Payments*, London: Allen & Unwin.

Frenkel, J.A. and Johnson, H.G. (eds) (1978), *The Economics of Exchange Rates*, Reading, Mass: Addison-Wesley.

Friedman, M. (1956), 'The Quantity Theory of Money, A Restatement', in M. Friedman (ed.), *Studies in the Quantity Theory of Money*, Chicago: University of Chicago Press.

Friedman, M. (1968), 'The Role of Monetary Policy', *American Economic Review*, March.

Friedman, M. (1974), *Monetary Correction* (IEA Occasional Paper No. 41), London: Institute of Economic Affairs.

Friedman, M. (1975), *Unemployment Versus Inflation? An Evaluation of the Phillips Curve* (IEA Occasional Paper No. 44), London: Institute of Economic Affairs.

Friedman, M. (1977), 'Inflation and Unemployment', *Journal of Political Economy*, June.

Friedman, M. and Schwartz, A.J. (1963), *A Monetary History of the United States, 1867–1960*, Princeton: Princeton University Press.

Hall, S.G., Henry, S.B. and Wilcox, S.B. (1989), 'The Long-Run Determinants of the UK Monetary Aggregates' (Bank of England Discussion Paper No. 41).

Hendry, D.F. and Mizon, G.E. (1978), 'Serial Correlation as a Convenient Simplification, Not a Nuisance. A Comment on a Study of the Demand for Money by the Bank of England', *Economic Journal*, September.

Henry, S.G.B. and Ormerod, P.A. (1978), 'Incomes Policy and Wage Inflation: Empirical Evidence for the U.K. 1961–1977', *National Institute Economic Review*, August.

Hicks, J.R. (1950), *A Contribution to the Theory of the Trade Cycle*, Oxford: Oxford University Press.

Holden, K., Peel, D.A. and Thompson, J.L. (1985), *Expectations: Theory and Evidence*, London: Macmillan.

Holden, K., Peel, D.A. and Thompson, J.L. (1991), *Economic Forecasting*, Cambridge: Cambridge University Press.

Johnson, H.G. (1972), 'The Monetary Approach to Balance of Payments Theory', in H.G. Johnson (ed.), *Further Essays in Monetary Economics*, London: Macmillan.

Keynes, J.M. (1936), *The General Theory of Employment, Interest and Money*, London: Macmillan.

Klamer, A. (1984), *The New Classical Macroeconomics*, Brighton: Wheatsheaf Books.

Kmenta, J. (1986), *Elements of Econometrics*, London: Macmillan.

Kydland, F.E. and Prescott, E.C. (1980), 'A Competitive Theory of Fluctuations and the Feasibility and Desirability of Stabilisation Policy', in S. Fischer (ed.), *Rational Expectations and Economic Policy*, Chicago: University of Chicago Press.

Laidler, D.E.W. (1981), 'Monetarism: An Interpretation and an Assessment', *Economic Journal*, March.

Laidler, D.E.W. (1982), *Monetarist Perspectives*, Oxford: Philip Allan.

Laidler, D.E.W. (1985), *The Demand for Money: Theories, Evidence and Problems*, 3rd edition, New York: Harper & Row.

Laidler, D.E.W. (1986), 'The New Classical Contribution to Macroeconomics', *Banca Nazionale Del Lavoro Quarterly Review*, March.

Laidler, D.E.W. (1990), *Taking Money Seriously*, Oxford: Philip Allan.

Leijonhufvud, A. (1968), *On Keynesian Economics and the Economics of Keynes*, Oxford: Oxford University Press.

Lipsey, R.G. (1960), 'The Relationship between Unemployment and the Rate of Change of Money Wage Rates in the U.K. 1862–1957: A Further Analysis', *Economica*, February.

Lucas, R.E. (1973), 'Some International Evidence on Output–Inflation Trade-Offs', *American Economic Review*, June.

Lucas, R.E. (1975), 'An Equilibrium Model of the Business Cycle', *Journal of Political Economy*, December.

Lucas, R.E. (1977), 'Understanding Business Cycles', in K. Brunner and A.H. Meltzer (eds), *Stabilization of the Domestic and International Economy*, Amsterdam and New York: North-Holland.

Maddock, R. and Carter, M. (1982), 'A Child's Guide to Rational Expectations', *Journal of Economic Literature*, March.

McCulloch, J.H. (1975), 'The Monte-Carlo Cycle in Business Activity', *Economic Inquiry*, September.

Mintz, I. (1969), *Dating Postwar Business Cycles* (NBER Occasional Paper No. 107), New York.

Modigliani, F. (1977), 'The Monetarist Controversy, or Should We Forsake Stabilization Policies?', *American Economic Review*, March.

Mullineux, A.W. (1984), *The Business Cycle after Keynes*, Brighton: Wheatsheaf Books.

Mundell, R.A. (1962), 'The Appropriate Use of Monetary and Fiscal Policy for Internal and External Balance', *IMF Staff Papers*, 9.

Mundell, R.A. (1963), 'Capital Mobility and Stabilisation Policy under Fixed and Flexible Exchange Rates', *Canadian Journal of Economics and Political Science*, vol. 29, no. 4.

Mussa, M. (1976), 'The Exchange Rate, the Balance of Payments and Monetary and Fiscal Policy under a Regime of Controlled Floating', *Scandinavian Journal of Economics*, 78.

Muth, J.F. (1961), 'Rational Expectations and the Theory of Price Movements', *Econometrica*, July.

Ott, D.J. and Ott, A.F. (1965), 'Budget Balance and Equilibrium Income', *Journal of Finance*, March.

Phelps, E.S. (1967), 'Phillips Curves, Expectations of Inflation, and Optimal Unemployment over Time', *Economica*, August.

Phelps, E.S. (1968), 'Money Wage Dynamics and Labour Market Equilibrium', *Journal of Political Economy*, August.

Phillips, A.W. (1958), 'The Relation between Unemployment and the Rate of Change of Money Wage Rates in the United Kingdom, 1861–1957', *Economica*, November.

Radcliffe Committee (1959), *Committee on the Working of the Monetary System: Report*, Cmnd 827, London: HMSO.

Samuelson, P.A. (1939), 'Interaction between the Multiplier Analysis and the Principle of Acceleration', *Review of Economics and Statistics*, May.

Sargent, T.J. (1986), *Rational Expectations and Inflation*, New York: Harper & Row.

Sargent, T.J. and Wallace, N. (1975), 'Rational Expectations, the Optimal Monetary Instrument and the Optimal Money Supply Rule', *Journal of Political Economy*, April.

Sargent, T.J. and Wallace, N. (1985), 'Some Unpleasant Monetarist Arithmetic', *Federal Reserve Bank of Minneapolis Quarterly Review*, Winter.

Shaw, G.K. (1984), *Rational Expectations: An Elementary Exposition*, Brighton: Wheatsheaf Books.

Stein, J.L. (1982), *Monetarist, Keynesian and New Classical Economics*, Oxford: Basil Blackwell.

Stevenson, A., Muscatelli, V. and Gregory, M. (1988), *Macroeconomic Theory and Stabilisation Policy*, Oxford: Philip Allan.

Thompson, J.L. (1988), *A Financial Model of the UK Economy*, Aldershot: Avebury.

Tobin, J. (1956), 'The Interest Elasticity of Transactions Demand for Cash', *Review of Economics and Statistics*, August.

Tobin, J. (1958), 'Liquidity Preference as Behaviour towards Risk', *Review of Economic Studies*, February.

Tobin, J. (1972), 'Inflation and Unemployment', *American Economic Review*, March.

Vane, H.R. and Thompson, J.L. (1979), *Monetarism: Theory, Evidence and Policy*, Oxford: Martin Robertson.

Author Index

Subject Index